SAM STEELE AND THE NORTHWEST REBELLION

The Trail of 1885

WAYNE F. BROWN

HERITAGE

VICTORIA · VANCOUVER · CALGARY

Heritage House Publishing Company Ltd.
heritagehouse.ca

Library and Archives Canada Cataloguing in Publication
Brown, Wayne
    Sam Steele and the Northwest Rebellion: the trail of 1885 / Wayne Brown.

(Amazing stories)
Includes bibliographical references and index.
Also issued in electronic format.
ISBN 978-1-927527-22-1

    1. Riel Rebellion, 1885. 2. Steele, Samuel B. (Samuel Benfield), 1848-1919. 3. North West Mounted Police (Canada)—Biography. I. Title. II. Series: Amazing stories (Victoria, BC)

FC3215.B76 2013   971.05'4   C2013-900031-3

Series editor: Lesley Reynolds
Proofreader: Liesbeth Leatherbarrow

Cover photo: Sam Steele, photographed by Hegg & Company, Dawson, Yukon, in 1898. Courtesy of the Sir Samuel Steele Collection (http://steele.library.ualberta.ca), Bruce Peel Special Collections Library, University of Alberta (2008.1.2.1.6.1.12).

The interior of this book was produced on 30% post-consumer recycled paper, processed chlorine free and printed with vegetable-based inks.

Heritage House acknowledges the financial support for its publishing program from the Government of Canada through the Canada Book Fund (CBF), Canada Council for the Arts and the province of British Columbia through the British Columbia Arts Council and the Book Publishing Tax Credit.

 Canadian Patrimoine Heritage canadien   Canada Council Conseil des Arts for the Arts du Canada   BRITISH COLUMBIA ARTS COUNCIL

17 16 15 14 13 1 2 3 4 5
Printed in Canada

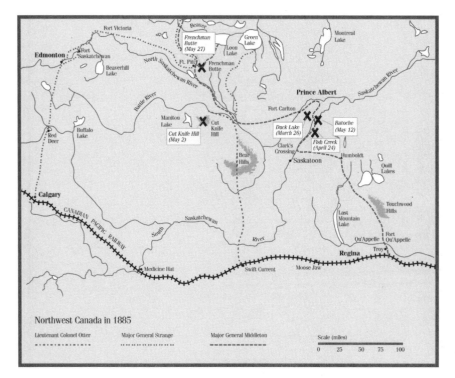

Major places and events of the Northwest Rebellion. TOM HOWELL

Contents

Prologue

PINNED DOWN BY THE CREE, *the three Scouts fired blindly into the night, not knowing if their shots were having any effect on the enemy. Shouting warnings and cursing loudly, Sam Steele, Joe Butlin and Tom McClelland fired and reloaded again and again. The mounted Cree seemed to be everywhere, and the Scouts knew they were in trouble. Where was the trailing rear guard that should have arrived to protect them?*

Sam Steele had been warned that Cree were lurking near the confluence of Pipestone Creek and the North Saskatchewan River, but the weary members of Steele's Scouts needed rest. As Steele and his two trusted companions went ahead to scout out a campsite, followed at a distance by a rear guard of two other Scouts, they warily rode along the bank of Pipestone Creek, watching and listening intently in the midnight darkness. Finally satisfied that they had found a safe place to camp and rest the men and horses, the three riders turned to head back to the main column of Scouts.

Bang! Out of the darkness came a deafening noise and a fiery blaze of orange. An ambush! The Scouts struggled to control their horses and frantically groped for their guns. As a Cree warrior dashed from his hiding place toward his horse, Butlin fired, hitting his fleeing target. But now more muzzle flashes were coming out of the darkness. Now dismounted and surrounded, the desperate Scouts knew they were in trouble. They returned fire as fast as they could lever new cartridges into their Winchesters.

The attack had happened so quickly that there had been no time for their rear guard to charge to their aid as planned. It seemed an eternity since the first shots had shattered the midnight silence. Where were they?

Introduction

THE LIVES OF FIRST NATIONS people in Western Canada underwent tumultuous changes between 1700 and 1885. They moved from the bow and arrow to the Industrial Revolution, a "step forward" foisted on all indigenous people in North America by the white man's colonization. Three factors in particular had a monumental effect on Aboriginal culture in the West during that era: the acquisition of the firearm; the introduction of the horse; and, most significant, the extermination of the buffalo, which nearly destroyed the indigenous culture of the Canadian prairies.

For eons, the plains Natives lived as hunter-gatherers who depended on the great buffalo herds roaming the prairies as their primary food source. The buffalo not only provided them with food, it also supplied clothing, shelter and tools. With a seemingly unending supply of buffalo to provide the necessities of life, there was limited conflict between tribes. The intrusion of the white man and the consequent introduction of firearms and horses upset this delicate balance, and life on the prairies changed dramatically. Not all tribes acquired firearms or horses at the same time, thus a domino effect developed as well-armed, highly mobile tribes gained the advantage and drove off any weaker tribes existing adjacent to them. These weaker tribes were forced to move into other tribes' territories, displacing them through yet more conflict. This displacement spread from east to west in Canada, and to some extent into the North, where the gun was an integral part of the fur trade.

Horses descended from the Spanish conquistadors' mounts appeared in Canada about 1730, and as these beasts of burden became more available, life on the prairies changed significantly. The traditional teepee expanded from about a 3-metre radius to double that size, as it now could be transported by a horse-drawn travois. In addition, a warrior easily could travel 70 to 80 kilometres a day on horseback, while a man on foot covered 40 kilometres. It's no wonder that horses came to symbolize wealth, while guns earned—for good or bad—respect.

Until the last decades of the 19th century, a traveller—white or Native—could rely on the buffalo as the single source of necessities during an extended trip across western

Canada, and many of the early explorers did just that. Even as late as the Palliser Expedition of 1858–60, travellers often were hampered from continuing their journey by massive herds of buffalo that sometimes took days to pass their campsites. By 1880, only 20 years later, there were virtually no buffalo left on the Great Plains of North America. Native hunters were reduced to killing small game in a desperate attempt to ward off starvation and relied on trading anything of value or resorting to theft to acquire clothing, shelter and tools, all of which had been provided by the buffalo in the past. The culture of raiding grew, conducted much like a form of gang activity, as mounted, armed raiding parties scoured nearly every corner of the plains.

In Ottawa, Sir John A. Macdonald and his government understood the dilemma caused by the decline of the buffalo herds and foresaw the potentially disastrous consequences they would face if the starving Natives challenged the government's authority. The government's solution was to confine Native people to designated Indian Reserves and then to teach them agriculture—by force, if necessary. A series of treaties to acquire land from once-nomadic Natives was initiated. The land would be relinquished in exchange for services to be provided by the government. Some treaties had been signed years before, such as the Selkirk Treaty of 1817 in Manitoba, but most of the prairie tribes remained to be dealt with. Macdonald appointed Alexander Morris, the politically loyal Lieutenant-Governor of Manitoba and the North-West Territories, to venture west and complete the remaining treaties with the plains tribes. Between 1872 and 1876, he presided over the negotiations and signing of Treaties 3, 4, 5 and 6. Early in the fall of 1876, the last treaty—Treaty 6—was signed in two locations: Fort Carlton and Fort Pitt. Sam Steele was part of the ceremonial contingent of North West Mounted Police (NWMP) who participated in these two historic events.

It was originally planned that all the Cree bands would gather at Fort Carlton for the negotiations and signing of Treaty 6. Some of these bands resided far to the west near Whitefish Lake and Saddle Lake, while Big Bear's band had recently moved into the Frog Lake area. These bands were reluctant to attend, using the long travelling distances as an excuse not to participate. The remedy provided by the government was to split the signing locations, with a second gathering planned for early September at Fort Pitt.

The Cree, deeply concerned over the proposed agreement, sought out and paid an interpreter to represent them in the treaty negotiations. The man they chose was Peter Erasmus, a Metis free trader from Whitefish Lake. Highly respected, impeccably honest, well-educated and fully conversant in both Cree and English, he was clearly the best man for the job. Peter represented his employers superbly, patiently going through the details of the treaty document point by point. He diligently explained and discussed the contents with the Cree councils to ensure they fully understood the ramifications of the white man's words. Many of the Cree leaders, especially Big Bear, were unhappy with the deal, foreseeing the dangers that lay in the specific conditions that Erasmus identified. Treaty 6 was clearly unfair, yet there was little choice but to sign. Refusing to do so meant cold, slow starvation, but even so, Big Bear stalled for time and did not sign until December 1882. The treaty's specific terms soon began to breed discontent and distrust among the Natives. Like a cauldron brewing, the swelling wrath would eventually erupt in a boiling froth of murder.

A similar predicament emerged with the Metis in Batoche, Saskatchewan. The Metis were neither Indian nor white, but of mixed blood, and they existed in a unique separate culture. The first Metis uprising began in 1869 at Red River, when Louis Riel, an astute Metis politician, led a group of political dissidents against Ottawa by forming a provisional government. For some months, Riel negotiated with the federal government over the terms of the Red River Colony's entry into Confederation, but in March 1870, he ordered the execution of Thomas Scott, an Irish Protestant who had been convicted of rebelling against Riel's government. As a result of Scott's death and continuing unrest at Fort Garry, Ottawa sent a military force west in the summer of 1870 under Colonel Garnet Wolseley to suppress the Red River Rebellion and enforce federal authority. Marching as part of Wolseley's military force was none other than a young Sam Steele, in the West for the first time and loving the experience.

Much of the Metis dissatisfaction was with the English system of surveying the territory. The French Metis were familiar with the seigneurial system from New France (Quebec) which featured strips of property running parallel to each other, back from the riverbank. This system provided each landowner with water access, highly valued in the day of the canoe. The English system being imposed on them was what we are familiar with today: townships and sections laid out in a series of squares with no regard to geographical features. Adding to the discontent were a number of other politically driven factors, including Metis resentment toward the domineering policies of the Hudson's Bay Company (HBC), and Lord Selkirk's settlement. The rebellion was quelled with military intervention and failed in most respects, but to Louis Riel's credit, it had resulted in the creation of the Province of Manitoba.

Many disgruntled Red River Metis dispersed across the prairies after the collapse of their provisional government, moving to small but growing enclaves at Batoche, St. Albert, Lac La Nonne and St. Paul de Metis. Fourteen years later, the buffalo were gone and the life of the independent-minded Metis would never be the same. Alienation toward Ottawa's rule continued to simmer, mostly over the same issues as before, but eventually neared the boiling point. Led by Gabriel Dumont, a delegation of Metis from Batoche travelled to Montana, where Louis Riel was living after fleeing from Canada in the summer of 1870. Dumont convinced Riel to come back to Canada and lead his people for the second time. He agreed to return, and on his triumphant arrival in Batoche in July 1884 he immediately began to organize the Metis, forming another provisional government with the intent of battling an insensitive, overbearing government in Ottawa. This was the prelude to the 1885 Northwest Rebellion.

The rebellion involved three separate conflicts, beginning with Louis Riel and the Metis at Batoche. When political avenues failed, Riel's armed force, led by Gabriel Dumont, confronted the NWMP at the battle of Duck Lake on March 26, 1885. This battle was soon followed by the murder of at least nine people by Wandering Spirit's Cree faction to the west, at Frog Lake on April 2. The third conflict occurred west of Fort Battleford at Cutknife Hill with a pre-emptive strike by Lieutenant Colonel Otter's force against Chief Poundmaker's Cree on May 2. There was some limited communication between the rebel factions involved in the three conflicts but never any organized co-ordination between them.

The supreme commander of the government forces was General Frederick Middleton, who directed his own force and the two others led by General Thomas Bland "Jingo" Strange and Colonel William Otter during the campaign to quell the rebellion. Middleton personally commanded the militia forces in two confrontations with the Metis—Tourond's Coulee (Fish Creek) and the four-day battle at Batoche.

Back in Ottawa, Prime Minister Macdonald's years

in office had not been easy ones. He had brokered Confederation, been defeated at the polls and was then re-elected. In 1871, the Macdonald government had convinced British Columbia to join Confederation with the promise to connect the new province to the rest of Canada by rail. The fulfillment of that promise had been stalled. Meanwhile, the Boundary Commission had diligently surveyed and defined the southern border between Canada and the United States, establishing the border along the 49th parallel in hopes of protecting the integrity of the new nation from American intrusion. In 1881, to satisfy his promise to BC, Macdonald launched into building a rail line across the country. The Canadian Pacific Railway (CPR) was his "national dream," a ribbon of steel that would bind Canada together.

By early 1885, Macdonald was confronted with an imminent rebellion of Metis and Natives on the prairies. The likelihood of a general war erupting grew as each day passed. Then a revelation struck him—a war! What better way to justify this yet-to-be completed rail line than to fight a war, demonstrating the railway's value by moving Canadian troops quickly to the front?

1

Forward March

ON APRIL 11, 1885, SAM STEELE, North West Mounted Police officer extraordinaire, was back in Calgary, having just got off the CPR train running east from end of track near Golden, BC. He stood before retired British general Thomas Bland "Jingo" Strange in a room in the NWMP barracks at the east end of Stephen Avenue. Steele was the epitome of a Mountie, immaculate in his chalk-white helmet and scarlet tunic. His dark blue pants with the distinctive yellow stripe were neatly tucked inside polished black boots.

Steele was renowned as a highly competent trouble-shooter within the NWMP. His career had included nearly every pivotal event in the early history of the Scarlet Force, from the time it was formed in 1873–74. Steele had signed on the third line of the initial roster and was issued badge number 5. He spent most of his early months in the fledgling force training other recruits to ride a horse with dignity—back erect and chin up. Along with his two brothers, Richard and Godfrey, he endured the Great March West of the NWMP as part of Inspector W.D. Jarvis's column that travelled along the Carlton Trail to Edmonton.

Steele's six-foot frame featured solid, square shoulders, a burly chest and a football player's arms and legs. Virtually inexhaustible, he possessed a "let's get it done without fuss" attitude. He was no stuffed shirt but exhibited a supreme confidence in himself, regardless of the circumstances. With the exception of a few jealous officers in the higher ranks, he was admired by nearly every member of the force.

"Jingo" Strange—the nickname came from his days serving in India—sat behind his orderly desk, poring over a letter. He glanced up, put a sheet of paper on the top of a neat stack and leaned back. As he removed a monocle from his eye, he waved Steele to a chair. The conversation went something like this: "Steele, glad you could get here so quickly. Sit down man. Things don't look good right now, so I'd better bring you up to date. Superintendent Crozier over at Fort Carlton had a scrap about two weeks ago with that Metis agitator Riel, and he nearly got himself and his men whipped. Crozier's in Prince Albert right now and reported over a dozen casualties and a number of men wounded. Happened on March 26 when he went to close out a local

Samuel Benfield Steele, photographed in 1890, wears his Northwest Rebellion medal with the Saskatchewan clasp across the ribbon, indicating he served in combat.

PROVINCIAL ARCHIVES OF ALBERTA, B.1968

store at Duck Lake and remove its supplies before the Metis could get at them. They had a rough time of it, I gather. Then on April 2, some Cree killed at least nine settlers and two of the priests, God keep them, and took the women prisoners at Frog Lake, near Fort Pitt. We haven't had any telegraph messages from Inspector Dickens at Fort Pitt since April 3, and I hope it was just the line going down again. Fort Battleford is in a bad way too. Chief Poundmaker's warriors are running wild, and the fort is virtually under siege. Colonel Otter is marching north right now from Fort Qu'Appelle to relieve them.

"It appears the entire country is on the verge of erupting into a full-scale war, and we have to get it under control—and soon. I'm expecting the first battalion of militia forces to arrive here from the east on the train tomorrow, with more to come in the days ahead. Locally, we've formed the Rocky Mountain Rangers with Major Stewart in command and Kootenay Brown from Waterton Lakes leading them when they patrol the southern regions of the territory from the mountains east to Fort Qu'Appelle. They'll be displaying a military presence on the plains to prevent local Natives from getting any ideas. Colonel Walker will command the Calgary Home Guard and provide security for our local residents while a lot of the men are away on duty.

"I have a job for you too, Sam, and it's dangerous. I need you to form an advance-reconnaissance scouting group for my command, the Alberta Field Force. You and your men will be on your own, only communicating with me by messenger. You'll ride a day or so ahead of the main column as we advance; first to Edmonton, then east, down the North Saskatchewan River to deal with these renegades. I've already designated your command to Ottawa as 'Steele's

Scouts. My old East India war comrade, General Middleton, is our commander-in-chief, and he plans to advance on the Metis at Batoche as soon as he can march there. Otter is to gain and reinforce Battleford, while it will be our responsibility to flush out the Cree around Fort Pitt. We must, above all, free the captured women; in the meantime, God keep them safe."

The two men then launched into a discussion of the details. Steele and his NWMP members would be temporarily transferred into the militia, Steele with a rank of major. He believed roughly 60 scouts would be sufficient for his force; he'd use many of his dependable NWMP members from the CPR railhead, plus an equal number of experienced, local ex-military veterans and reliable, savvy, cowboy volunteers. Strange dictated that the NWMP members, riding in a stealthy scouting role, should wear their conspicuous bright red jackets inside out. Steele instantly refused, saying, "Sir, with respect, my men are not turncoats!"

Strange paused; they both realized the humour in the statement and together laughed it off. Strange relented, saying, "Well, put them in buckskins, or they can wear their brown stable jackets then." Steele would be the only one to wear the charismatic red tunic, insisting on that concession. As troop commander, he chose a white cowboy hat, even though Strange thought Steele would get himself shot for it.

In short order, Steele enlisted 42 men: 22 Alberta Mounted Rifles and 20 volunteer cowboys from Calgary to augment his NWMP detachment from the railhead. Others would be added to the roster later in Edmonton— eager volunteers such as his two brothers, Richard and Godfrey, as well as the legendary "fighting preacher," Reverend George McKay.

The NWMP members of the Scouts felt their status was above the "lowly cowboys" and wore their yellow-striped pants to identify themselves to others as police. Most retained their issue sidearms and were given brand-new Winchester 45-75 rifles, (45 is the calibre, 75 is the measure in grains of gunpowder which propels the bullet), along with an initial issue of 300 rounds of ammunition. The rifle was carried in a unique thong-style holster, suspended from the saddle horn so the gun rested crosswise in front of the rider and could be brought into action quickly. Because stealth would be important, all their equipment and horse tack was carefully modified to prevent clinking and jingling while they were on the move. But while their gear was quickly made ready, the horses were another matter. The tough, prairie-raised, half-wild mustangs still required training to bring them under control enough to be acceptable mounts.

All members of the Alberta Field Force, including the infantry soldiers, were issued protective brown cowboy hats, replacing their normal headgear of dinky pillbox hats and military wedge caps. Concerned that distinguishing each other from the enemy might become a problem, especially with the Scouts wearing buckskin jackets similar to what their enemy might wear, Strange instructed the entire force, including the security contingents patrolling the southern plains, to pin the brim of their hats up on the left side so that the force's members could easily be identified, especially during any skirmishes.

The day after Steele arrived in Calgary, the 65th Mount Royal Rifles, a French-speaking regiment, arrived by train from Quebec, marched down Stephen Avenue and set up camp on the river flats next to the old grounds of Fort Calgary. On April 17, five days later, the 92nd Winnipeg Light Infantry arrived and marched into camp to continue their combat training. Most of the young volunteers in both battalions were completely inexperienced young men from the city out on "a great adventure." Many of the green soldiers had never marched in order, much less fired a gun, even for fun. This provided many a comical situation as they stumbled and crashed about, learning their left arm from the right on the parade square. Their marksmanship on the firing range proved atrocious, which provided entertainment for some curious locals. With little else to do, these citizens spent their time lounging at the gun range and parade square, scrutinizing the recruits' pathetic abilities. The greenhorn soldiers were amazed at the marksmanship the cowboy members of the Scouts demonstrated in practice. The cowboys rode full tilt with pistol or rifle at the ready and put a bullet into or very close to the target's bull's eye nearly every time.

By April 20, it became imperative the Alberta Field Force begin their march north; however, much of the expected equipment and armaments had not yet arrived in Calgary on the train. Major Hatton's Alberta Mounted Rifles didn't even have saddles for their horses. Consequently, Strange was forced to leave nearly a third of his force behind as they waited to be outfitted; they would simply have to catch up later. Despite this frustrating limitation, the force began forming up at about noon, but many of the Steele's Scouts' horses were still uncomfortable with the close quarters when they formed into ranks, and the unfamiliar noises spooked many of them into bucking off their riders. Strange, a powerless witness to this impromptu rodeo, simply shook his head in utter disbelief. It took until nearly 4 PM for the bugler to finally sound the advance.

Flanked by Sam Steele and his Scouts, General Strange led the column, followed by his personal wagon with his driver and cook, Wheeler Michael, whose homemade, diminutive Union Jack fluttered in the afternoon breeze from the buggy whip. The force faced its first challenges when it crossed the Bow River in high water at the sawmill's ford in Eau Claire, then climbed out of the river valley up the steep Centre Street hill. The original Edmonton Trail had meandered westward from Calgary almost to Cochrane before turning northward, but the Alberta Field Force would follow a more direct route toward Edmonton that would eliminate miles of unnecessary travel.

The column forded Nose Creek near today's Calgary International Airport. The clay stream bank proved exceedingly slippery, giving men and animals alike a taste of the stream-crossing challenges to come. The first night's camp was set up near the Nose Creek crossing to allow the men to dry out their equipment. The next morning, reveille was sounded at 4:30 AM, and the day's march took them to the mouth of McPherson's Coulee, just a couple of kilometres north of Airdrie. That night the force huddled in their canvas tents, shivering through a severe spring blizzard with temperatures dipping so low they had to chip the tent pegs out of the frozen ground in the morning. Regardless of the weather, they continued north, marching at a superb pace and covering about 19 to 20 kilometres each day.

While General Strange marched northward, General Frederick Middleton, the supreme commander of the forces sent to suppress the rebellion, had marched overland from Fort Qu'Appelle and faced the Metis forces of Louis Riel on April 23 at what was then identified as Fish Creek. (Today this historic site is known as Tourond's Coulee.) This confrontation resulted in a stalemate. The militia had attempted to utilize their field gun, but the barrel couldn't be depressed enough to fire on the Metis deployed below. Captain James Peters of the Royal Canadian Artillery took photos of this event with a portable hand camera; these photographs are the first ever taken of Canadian forces in conflict. Citing his casualties of 6 dead and nearly 50 wounded as the reason,

Middleton delayed in his camp for two weeks after the confrontation. Although Middleton's forces had not actually been defeated, it was not the auspicious beginning to the campaign he had hoped for.

As the Alberta Field Force proceeded north, General Strange enforced strict rules. Despite the British military custom of issuing each man a healthy tot of rum every evening after the day's march, Strange allowed no alcohol among the soldiers. In addition, there would be no discharge of firearms for any reason other than by order; this was to ensure that a hostile attack would be recognized immediately. To enforce the order, ammunition was withheld from the marching soldiers until they reached Red Deer. On April 25, the skies cleared, the sun came out and a chinook began blowing from the west. John Corryell, an ex-military captain, and several others developed snow blindness from the bright sun reflecting off the snow. Corryell was so afflicted that he required one of his men to guide him until his sight recovered.

With the hectic pace, Steele and his Scouts rode at a gallop much of the time, trying to stay ahead of the main column. They ferreted out the route, identified possible dangerous ambush sites and determined the coming night's campsite. A prairie fire had burned through the region two weeks before, so there was little firewood to be found and no grass for grazing the horses; instead the riders had to rely on feed brought along in the freight wagons. As the day progressed, a warm wind melted the snow, revealing a charred, blackened landscape and provoking a foreboding, eerie sense of desolation among the soldiers. In general, the route chosen by the Alberta Field Force was approximately that of the old Highway 2 as it makes its way to Edmonton. The force passed close to Didsbury, Olds and Innisfail and finally approached the Red Deer River just west of Red Deer.

The Alberta Field Force reached the river ford in the late afternoon of April 25 and bivouacked on the south bank in anticipation of crossing the swollen stream the next day. There was great apprehension in the air, since the opposite side of the river appeared to be a perfect setting for an enemy ambush. The Scouts went across first but had great difficulty penetrating the thick willows along the riverbanks, so they couldn't guarantee the opposite bank was clear. In the distance, smoke signals drifted up from the hilltops, suggesting hostile forces were lurking there, possibly bent on attacking when the militia was crossing the river and at its most vulnerable. General Strange countered the potential danger by loading a company of fully armed volunteers into several wagons to make the spearhead fording attempt. Strange climbed into the first wagon and led the crossing himself, a feat accomplished without incident. Once the initial fording had been completed, a doubled guard was stationed for protection until the main force crossed the following day.

Once the entire force had crossed the river, Strange

ordered a contingent of 20 soldiers of the 65th Mount Royal Rifles, under Lieutenant Bedard Normandeau, to remain behind. They would protect the crossing by building and manning a fortress capable of warding off any hostile attack. General Strange allowed Normandeau to name this new fortification after himself. At the next crossing, at the Battle River, Fort Ostell was constructed from the looted HBC post, and Fort Ethier was constructed and manned in a similar manner on Bigstone Creek. In the end, none of these three fortifications saw any notable action, although they were all allegedly sniped at on occasion, but the control of these vulnerable river crossings was critically important for the protection of supply wagon trains that would follow the force later.

Here at the Red Deer River, Reverend George McKay caught up with the Scouts. On hearing of the campaign against the rebels, he had thrown his bible, bedroll, pistol, rifle, some ammunition and a few clothes into his saddle bags and galloped off northward from Fort Macleod to join in the adventure. Steele, aware of McKay's reputation and fluency in Cree, instantly accepted the gun-toting preacher, appointing him as the Scouts' chaplain. He would serve the Scouts well in the weeks to come.

The Alberta Field Force advanced northward into the established First Nations Reserves near Hobbema. Several of the area chiefs were plainly sympathetic to the rebel cause and clearly resented the white settlers, so Strange decided to put on a show of authority. For their "edification," he ordered the marching militia to form up in closed ranks with fixed bayonets. With rifles at the slope, the soldiers quick marched through the collection of teepees set along the trail. This act of authority suitably impressed the dissident chiefs and others present, helping to demonstrate the immense power of the Great White Queen and deterring any belligerency.

From Hobbema, the column continued on, marching on the trail that led down the Mill Creek ravine to the banks of the North Saskatchewan River. There they used John Walter's ferry to cross the river to Edmonton on May 1. The force was welcomed with a traditional cannon salute from the old fort. Unfortunately, the excited gunners erred in loading the old fort's HBC relic, neglecting to remove the ramrod from the barrel prior to igniting the fuse. The cannon went off with a huge bang and a cloud of black powder smoke, its ramrod flying out across the river, never to be seen again.

The column proudly marched up the north bank of the river, past the old fort (situated where the Alberta Legislature is today) and into the townsite at the top of the valley. Just after the force arrived, a courier galloped in from Fort Saskatchewan carrying a request for assistance from NWMP inspector Arthur G. Griesbach. Through rumours and gossip, the community's residents had made themselves so anxious that a general alarm was triggered by the inspector's own house cat prowling about one dark night. General Strange responded by ordering a company of his militia to march downstream immediately to the community, quieting worries over a perceived rebel threat. As with the other militia personnel drop-offs, this tactical necessity further eroded the Alberta Field Force's ranks. At each key location, Strange ordered small companies of soldiers to remain behind to boost morale, augment local volunteers on guard and protect the militia's supply lines. Strange also assisted the local men in forming a Home Guard and advised them how to enhance their defences.

The Alberta Field Force was now halfway to its destination of Fort Pitt in the territory of Saskatchewan. After marching at an average rate of about 30 kilometres each day without incident, the hiatus in Edmonton provided an opportunity to further prepare the soldiers and scouts alike for what they would eventually face. It would also allow some of the delayed contingents from Calgary a chance to catch up.

CHAPTER

Downstream along the North Saskatchewan

GENERAL STRANGE AND THE Alberta Field Force, with Steele's Scouts on each flank, paraded down Edmonton's Jasper Avenue on May 1, an event so important it even emptied the drunks from the local saloons to witness the spectacle. For weeks, rumours had flourished that a rebel Metis or Native attack on the town was imminent, and tensions were running high in the community. The arrival of the Alberta Field Force brought significant relief to the residents, who now felt safer with an army in their midst.

The column marched to the racetrack in northeast Edmonton (located at today's Eaton's Centre area) where they established their temporary camp and training areas.

All of the troops, the Scouts included, took the much-needed time to continue their training and preparation. The Scouts still needed to work with their new horses, training them to come to a bugled feed call and firing pistol shots while they were eating to accustom them to gunfire. The mounts were also trained to lie on their side, sacrificing their bodies to protect a besieged rider during an attack. Steele recruited an additional 19 Scouts from Edmonton, mostly chosen for their knowledge of the country to the east and for their ability to speak the Cree language.

While the Alberta Field Force was in Edmonton, General Middleton finally broke camp at Tourond's Coulee and marched on the Metis stronghold of Batoche. As they approached Batoche, Middleton's scouts exchanged rifle fire with the Metis scouts, and on May 7, Middleton's full force deployed into positions south of the village. Middleton's plan was to use the paddlewheel steamboat *Northcote* as a diversion; however, while steaming downstream, *Northcote*'s smokestacks were ripped off by the local ferry's cable, which had been lowered by the Metis to damage the steamboat. Even though the militia had both a field gun and Gatling gun (an early version of the machine gun) at their disposal, the fighting resulted in a standoff. Finally, on the morning of May 12, after four days of structured attacks and Metis repulses, Colonel Williams led a determined company attack on his own initiative, overrunning the Metis positions and quickly ending the stalemate. With the collapse of the Metis at Batoche, General Middleton turned his men to march on Fort Battleford.

Back at Fort Edmonton, General Strange added nautical capability to his militia—five flat-bottomed river scows constructed of rough-hewn planks. The lead scow was huge—a full 32 metres long and 6 metres wide—and was aptly christened Big Bear. It was a true battleship, featuring the nine-pound field gun from Fort Macleod lashed down in the bow. Should the gun be needed, the scow could be rotated in the river current with the aid of its long sweeps (oars) and the gun brought to bear on any shore target. The smaller scows carried the soldiers, barricaded behind protective supplies. Built of new lumber, these vessels were difficult to waterproof, leaking badly until the joint caulking could swell sufficiently by absorbing river water.

The commanding officer of the 92nd Winnipeg Light Infantry, Colonel Smith, expressed grave concerns about the safety of these vessels and lodged an official written complaint. General Strange was compelled to convene a board of inquiry and hear out the complaint. Various experienced local boat builders and river-scow pilots testified that the crude vessels were safe for river use. The board agreed, so the task of loading continued, despite a late snow-and-rain storm on May 13. Even though the inquiry had found the vessels suitable for the journey, on the first day out, the scow carrying the horses sank in shallow water not far from Fort Saskatchewan. The lacklustre crew had neglected to bail seepage water out until it was too late, so they were relieved of their duty by Strange and replaced with more diligent personnel.

When the mounted Scouts passed by Fort Saskatchewan, two of Sam's brothers, Richard and Godfrey, joined him to serve as volunteer message couriers between Steele's land force and General Strange's river force. (A third brother, James, a schoolteacher, was forced to remain behind and lamented in his diary, "I'm hauling rails when I should be with the men.") Other Scouts were detailed to use canoes rather than ride on horseback, paddling ahead of the flotilla and searching out potential dangers that might lurk in the willows and underbrush on the banks of the North Saskatchewan.

By May 14, Steele and his Scouts had ranged out on patrol as far as Victoria Settlement, south of today's Smoky Lake, and ascertained that no threats existed to that point in the journey. General Strange, aboard a scow, paused at Victoria Settlement on May 16 where he learned by telegraph of the final charge at the Battle of Batoche. At this point he concluded it would be wise to foil the accompanying newspaper reporters who were bent on making his movements public in their newspapers. He feared they would jeopardize the force's effectiveness by providing information to the enemy through their publications. At the last minute, before casting off from Victoria Settlement, Strange switched the two regiments' positions, ordering the Winnipeg Light

Infantry to take to the land and march along the Carlton Trail. By keeping close to the telegraph line, they were able to communicate with General Middleton, even though the telegraph line also linked the press to the outside world. As they marched along the Carlton Trail in their red uniforms, the Winnipeg Light Infantry clearly displayed themselves as the queen's representatives to both hostile and friendly forces. Wearing dark green uniforms, the less conspicuous 65th Mount Royal Rifles occupied the scows drifting unobtrusively on the river.

The Alberta Field Force's short stay at Victoria Settlement coincided with the arrival of Cree chief Pakan, accompanied by two companions, Peter Erasmus and Peter Shirt. Their story, now a Cree legend, is part of the reason the rebellion remained a localized event that did not find favour among First Nations tribes on the southern prairies of Saskatchewan and Alberta. Had Chief Pakan joined the rebellion, many other bands would have also done so and provoked a large-scale war throughout the West. The circumstance that motivated First Nations restraint is known as "the legend of the white horse."

Sometime around 1875, a young man called Peter Shirt lived on the Whitefish Lake reserve, south of Lac La Biche. One night, Shirt was restless and had a troubling dream. His dream grew in intensity until, in the midst of it, the Great Spirit came and beckoned, telling Peter to rise and come with him. Peter got up and followed the divine being to a luxurious grassy knoll. The valley he viewed below basked in sunshine, while dark, thunderous clouds filled with flashing bolts of lightning loomed to the east. The Great Spirit silently pointed into the valley below, where lines of white tents contrasted with the green grass and the threatening storm. Looking to the west, Peter could see lines of red-clad soldiers marching toward the tents. Peter was incredulous and asked the Great Spirit, "What does this mean? Is this the future? Will this come to pass?"

The Great Spirit replied, "This will come to pass when your white horse dies." Peter awoke from his sleep, quickly pulled on his coat and ran to see the wisest man he knew—Peter Erasmus, his uncle. He told Erasmus of his dream and queried him about what it meant, but Peter could only advise the young man that he would learn in time.

Years passed, and the dream faded from Peter's memory. In the early 1880s, he traded for a white horse, which became trapped in deep snow and died during the winter of 1885. One day in mid-May 1885, word passed through the community that two emissaries from the Metis had arrived from Batoche. A council meeting to hear them out was planned for that evening. Shirt, now realizing the significance of his old dream, went to Erasmus and told him the white horse was now dead, as had been foretold in his dream, and that its death heralded a potentially deadly conflict. Despite Erasmus's doubts, Shirt insisted he must attend the council and present the warning from his vision.

The two went before the council together and Shirt related his dream and explained its meaning. Chief Pakan believed Shirt completely and became alarmed over the divine message; as a result, he refused to join the rebellion.

The next day, one of the Metis emissaries, Louis Cardinal, was murdered. Chief Pakan, fearing Metis revenge for the killing, gathered his followers and sought safety by hiding his people in the bush. Once this was accomplished, Shirt, Erasmus and Chief Pakan made the journey to Victoria Settlement to seek protection from the soldiers. Upon arriving at the North Saskatchewan River, the trio gazed into the valley. Below them were lines of white tents and soldiers marching in red tunics, just as they had done in Shirt's dream. It had come true! Chief Pakan was escorted to meet with General Strange, and he pledged his allegiance to the Great White Queen, consequently avoiding any involvement in hostilities. His example helped prevent other First Nations from joining in the rebellion.

As the 65th Mount Royal Rifles left Victoria Settlement, the atmosphere was almost holiday-like on the scows as the French-Canadian boatmen sang traditional refrains while they manoeuvred their unwieldy craft in the current. The soldiers enjoyed leisurely lunches as they slowly drifted by the riverbank scenery. On one occasion, somewhere near the Saddle Lake Reserve, the flotilla came under light sniping by an unseen enemy. The scows put to shore immediately, and the excited 65th scrambled ashore and extended in skirmish order, ultimately confronting no one as they filtered through the underbrush.

Incidents like this raised the vigilance of the marching soldiers and Steele's Scouts to a new level. Around this time, Reverend George McKay became involved in a confrontation that proved danger did indeed lurk in the vicinity. The preacher was riding along a game trail and in the distance spotted three Natives coming in his direction. Dismounting, he waited in ambush alongside the trail, and when the Natives drew near, he leaped from concealment, his Winchester aimed directly at them. He barked at them in Cree, "Naki! Pakitina!" ("Halt! Put it down!"). Caught completely by surprise, the three dropped their rifles on the ground and surrendered. McKay collected their guns and marched them back to the main force of Scouts, where they were chained into one of the wagons. One of them, a Saddle Lake Cree called Windy Boy, later escaped by carrying the heavy iron ball and leg shackle in his arms. He managed to elude his captors and hobble back to Saddle Lake where his restraints were removed.

As the vanguard of the marching Winnipeg Light Infantry, the Scouts continued their reconnaissance of the Carlton Trail and reached the Saddle Lake Reserve farm on May 22. Strange noted in his memoirs that somewhere between Saddle Lake and his river-bound flotilla, a sniper's bullet went through the hat of one of Sam's brothers while he galloped along as a courier between the two forces. From there, they continued eastward to St. Paul de Metis

(St. Paul, Alberta) before veering southeast toward the old free-traders' post Dogrumphouse (Elk Point, Alberta), where they set up camp in a miserably cold drizzle near the creek's confluence with the North Saskatchewan River. The morning light saw the rain continuing, and everyone felt depressed. It was now Sunday, May 24, Queen Victoria's birthday, and General Strange sensed the need for a little lift in the soldiers' morale. At the conclusion of the regular Sunday church parade, he addressed the men, saying the weather might well be cold and depressing, and there would be no fireworks to celebrate the occasion, but he fully expected there would be plenty of action for them all, now they were in hostile territory. Being bilingual, Strange gave a portion of his speech in French, to the delight of the Montreal regiment, who felt more accepted as a result. The men quietly broke up, camp was struck and the Winnipeg Light Infantry marched out, while the 65th embarked in their scows, both continuing in an easterly direction.

Later in the afternoon, with extreme wariness, Steele's Scouts approached the remnants of the Frog Lake community and made a grisly discovery. With it came a grim duty. They found the dead, decomposing bodies of the victims of the April 2 massacre. General Strange's reports indicated that the bodies of two Roman Catholic priests were found, dismembered and identifiable only by their prayer beads, in the burned-out basement of the church. With them were two other victims, an unemployed French schoolteacher and a lay brother. Despite the record, history has ignored these two victims and three others: a woman whose dismembered body was discovered stuffed down a well; the illegitimate son of the resident farming instructor, John Delaney; and Delaney's Cree mistress. The bodies of the other male settlers were discovered lying where they fell. Six weeks after their deaths, all of the corpses were buried in shallow graves by the Scouts.

It would take over a century for the complete story of what happened on April 2, 1885, to be revealed. It appears that after an apprehensive night, the entire community had gathered in the Catholic Church for an Easter celebration. The Cree war chief, Wandering Spirit, who had assumed authority of the band while the aging Chief Big Bear was away hunting, proposed to take all the white settlers hostage in the hopes of negotiating a better deal than Treaty 6 had provided. The band had endured years of deprivation and hardship at the hands of domineering "government men" who provided few of the wonders promised by the treaty.

Herding the church congregation outside, Wandering Spirit ordered them all to go to the Cree camp, located about two kilometres north on Frog Creek. One of the white men, Thomas Quinn, a strong-minded, authoritative Indian Agent, defiantly refused. Wandering Spirit, his warrior integrity and authority publicly challenged, levelled his Winchester at Quinn and warned the man one last time, "I tell you to go—you go!" Then he pulled the trigger, killing Quinn instantly at point-blank range. This act initiated the infamous killing spree that claimed eight other male victims, according to the official count, and possibly four other unidentified individuals. Each was hunted down and executed; there would be no negotiations.

During the evening of May 24, the 65th Mount Royal Rifles landed for the night and camped at the mouth of Frog Creek on the North Saskatchewan. Some of the senior officers hiked up the stream to the small settlement to view the burned buildings, debris and the freshly dug graves of the victims. With permission from their officers, some of the soldiers in camp erected a huge cross on the hilltop overlooking their camp, dedicating it to those who had been murdered.

The Alberta Field Force now had a clear understanding of their mission and why they were here in the wilds of Canada's West. They also realized the danger faced by those taken captive from Frog Lake. Meanwhile, newspaper stories written about the events at Frog Lake were full of hideous, unsubstantiated claims that fuelled readers' imaginations as they contemplated the victims' fate. This led to public pressure on the federal government that trickled down through General Middleton to General Strange and to Sam Steele and his Scouts. In the days ahead, this pressure would influence how they would perform in putting an end to this "Saskatchewan Rebellion."

Early in the morning of May 25, the Scouts reached Fort Pitt and once again performed a woeful burial duty. The body of NWMP constable David Cowan was found

Shown here trading at Fort Pitt, Chief Big Bear (in centre of photo with plumed hat) was maligned as the Cree leader during the Northwest Rebellion but actually strove for a peaceful solution to the conflict. GLENBOW ARCHIVES NA-1323-4

sprawled on the ground beside the trail leading down the slope to Fort Pitt. His revolver, tunic and rifle were missing. In a macabre act, his heart had been hacked out of his chest and pegged on a stick beside his body. Reverend McKay drew out his bible, and as the sombre Scouts encircled the fresh grave, he held a short service for the fallen policeman. Strange ordered a squad to canvass the surrounding area, searching for more victims, but they found none.

Fort Pitt was in ruins. Most of the buildings had been burned to the ground, and looted goods and broken possessions were strewn about in the dirt. Sam Steele was standing at the riverboat landing in front of the remains of Fort Pitt when General Strange floated around the bend with the 65th Mount Royal Rifles. Steele quickly briefed him, informing him that he had already detailed Captain James Oswald and his party of advanced Scouts to establish camp on high land to the east so they could watch for the enemy down the North Saskatchewan River valley. The 65th disembarked from the scows, formed into ranks and marched from the landing up the slope to the west.

The soldiers set up their camp adjacent to the area traditionally used by nearly all of the visiting tribes since the first fort was built in 1829. The nearby creek provided a source of water, and the area was also open to breezes that deterred the mosquitoes and bulldogs (horseflies) that harassed people and horses. Setting up camp away from the fort would also minimize any interference with the Winnipeg Light Infantry, which would begin cleaning up the site and repairing the few salvageable buildings the next day. Steele selected an area apart from the rest of the force, setting up the Scouts' camp in a poplar grove on the ridge north of the fort's ruins. This camp would rarely be used since the Scouts were away in the saddle most of the time.

The ruins of "Ol' Pitt" would become the military's home base for the next two months. It would witness the paddlewheeled steamboats coming round the bend, whistles blasting, and tying up at the landing, where they unloaded their cargoes and men in support of both the Alberta Field Force and General Middleton's battalions.

CHAPTER

3

Closing In

OVER THE YEARS, FORT PITT had been two separate forts. The earliest was an HBC fort built by Patrick Small in 1829, situated on the north side of the river, as was the practice, halfway between Fort Carlton and Fort Edmonton. The fort served the HBC during the tumultuous time when mounted, rifle-carrying southern tribes routinely raided into the North Saskatchewan River territory of the Cree. It saw the coming and going of most of the prominent explorers and fur traders who ventured west and recorded valuable details of their experiences. After an accidental fire levelled the old fort, a new structure was built about 1874, two years prior to the Treaty 6 signing ceremonies. This second fort, often referred to only as Pitt by local Natives, was just a collection of unfortified buildings. The lack of any bastions, palisades and lookout towers proved significant in the events of 1885. Photos of this fort taken in the summer of 1884 by Cornelius Soule show what appears to be a palisade; however, it was only a board fence to keep animals out of the garden.

In early 1885, Fort Pitt housed a NWMP detachment of about 26 men under the command of Inspector Francis Dickens, son of English novelist Charles Dickens, who was responsible for Francis's well-intended nickname, "Chickenstalker," a moniker used disparagingly by the Cree. Six junior constables from the detachment were detailed to the Frog Lake community. Two days prior to the Frog Lake murders, the community had decided that the constables, under senior constable Ralph Sleigh, should return to Fort Pitt in the hope this would calm the excited young Cree warriors of Big Bear's band. They left by wagon on April 1, wisely taking most of the firearms and ammunition with them from both Dill's Store and the HBC store.

After the infamous events of April 2 at Frog Lake, the white prisoners were taken to the Cree camp. Numerous warrior councils were convened before it was decided to move everyone to Fort Pitt. The Cree intended to confront the white men at the fort and negotiate an exchange of their captives for desperately needed food and medicine.

During the week following the murders, Inspector Dickens was convinced something terrible had happened at

Frog Lake, but he still had no confirmable details. As the days passed, the tension grew, as did the number of false alarms. One night, a vigilant police sentry spotted three dark forms slipping toward the buildings through the moonlit shadows. As the unknown prowlers noiselessly crept closer, the recently recruited constable opened fire, missing his target but awakening everyone with a start. In a moment, the three intruders were identified. Generating a round of howling, tension-relieving laughter, three of the fort's pigs ran off as fast as their short legs would propel them, snorting loudly all the way.

Dickens finally ordered two of his constables, David Cowan and Clarence Loasby, both with only three years' experience, accompanied by civilian guide Henry Quinn, to ride to Frog Lake and determine the status of the settlement. He also swore in as special constables all civilians at the fort who were competent with firearms. This official act permitted him to issue NWMP firearms to those civilians, including Elizabeth, Amelia and Kitty McLean, the three daughters of the chief trader. When the McLean sisters were issued rifles, they became the first female members of the NWMP. The little ammunition available in the fort was doled out; the police were issued 40 rounds and civilian sentries given 18 rounds for their Snider-Enfield carbines. Arms were so limited that even the HBC trade guns (muzzleloading muskets) were employed, requisitioned from the HBC store. Sentry watches were changed every two hours, and a reassuring password was circulated every 15 minutes.

The three-member scouting party of Cowan, Loasby and Quinn left in the early afternoon of April 13, going west along the river before swinging north to Frog Lake. In choosing this route, they missed encountering the entire Cree camp, which was moving toward the fort on another trail to the north.

The three McLean women—Elizabeth, the eldest, and Amelia and Kitty, who were only teenagers—were taking their turns manning the loopholes cut in the walls of the fort's buildings. Elizabeth went upstairs to a second-storey window to serve her designated two-hour shift as lookout. It was almost 4 PM when Elizabeth called out the open window, "Riders on the ridge!" Everyone shifted their eyes to the western horizon and the height of land that loomed over the fort about a thousand metres away. The main access trail that led into Fort Pitt dropped from the top of this rise into a long grove of spruce and budding poplar trees that divided the slope in half. The trail swept through this wooded strip and exited at an angle, slanting downward to the south before bending its way around the perimeter of the fort to the main entrance, which, as was the custom, faced the river on the east side.

Over the previous 10 days, the occupants of the fort had worked hard preparing for any attack, but despite the best efforts of over 75 desperate workers who hurriedly improvised a palisade and two bastions, the fort was nowhere near defensible. A brand-new, unproven river scow rested inside the fort's entrance. In the northeast corner, the Union Jack fluttered lazily on the flagstaff above the HBC flag at the NWMP barracks. It was dead quiet; only the occasional spring crow cawed from the trees along the river.

The mounted Cree warriors—some 250 of them in full battle regalia and war paint—were spreading out along the ridgeline with a slow, deliberate pace. The defenders whispered to each other as they watched the spectacle unfold. Amelia and Kitty McLean's fingers found the gun triggers as they practised sighting on the still out-of-range targets. Firing a gun wasn't anything new for the McLean girls—their father had seen to that. As each of them grew old enough, he had made certain they became competent with both pistols and rifles, and under his tutelage they became good shots. Amelia was considered the crack shot of the family, and both Amelia and Kitty had been fierce competitors in the fort's rabbit shooting contest on Christmas Day in 1884. Still, the situation must have seemed unreal to them—under siege as newly sworn-in special constables of the NWMP, a police carbine in their hands and expecting a charge any moment.

The afternoon wore on, and the sun sank behind the ridge, about to set. There would be no Cree attack that night, but come dawn the danger for those besieged in the fort would undoubtedly be renewed. In the evening, delegations appeared in the open under a white flag for a variety of reasons, one Native even begging a blanket, and Chief

Trader William McLean diligently met with each. McLean was invited to a parlay on the spot at ten o'clock the next morning, an invitation he readily accepted in the hope he could negotiate a truce with the Cree. With luck, he would convince them to go back to Frog Lake. If necessary, he would agree to any demands they made that fell within his authority, including promising that their living conditions would be improved in the future.

The appointed time arrived and a determined, unarmed McLean—the Cree called him Straight Tongue for his honesty—along with his HBC interpreter, Francois Dufresne, climbed over the barricades and walked out to meet the similarly unarmed Cree peace delegation. After a cordial, almost friendly discussion, McLean was asked to join their council of chiefs at their camp, over the rise and out of sight of the fort. This was potentially an extremely dangerous situation, but despite the personal risk, McLean reluctantly agreed. He drew out his white handkerchief and, as previously arranged, shook it out and blew his nose. This signalled the fort that there had been a change of the meeting plans as they had understood them. McLean turned and gave a wave of confidence, then he and Dufresne walked up the slope with the Cree delegation, away from the safety of the fort. It would be a long, tension-filled day for the fort's defenders as they awaited word from the pair.

The Cree council was already assembled at the camp when McLean and Dufresne were ushered in. The circle of seven headmen, who were lesser chiefs, sat armed to the teeth and with their faces covered in war paint. McLean knew that showing any fear would be catastrophic, so he seated himself in the assembly and did his best to act as if they were trading. The circle of chiefs began the parlay with their ceremonial smudge-cleansing ritual. The pipe was passed and smoked by each member in turn, but the first time it went around, McLean was ignored. However, on the second round, Chief Big Bear himself interrupted the ceremony, saying to the council, "Straight Tongue must be respected when he is among us like this. He should smoke as well." This was a minor victory for McLean, and he gained confidence from it. He fully realized this negotiation process could be the deal of a lifetime, and the lives of every person in the fort depended on his success.

The first Cree to speak was Imassees, the eldest son of Big Bear, who rose and described the Cree situation. He spoke of the grievances that had grown ever since the buffalo were gone, and now, because they were living on the white man's reserve, they were poor, without even a single meal to eat. That was why they were fighting this fight. There must be change.

McLean stood up, and with Dufresne interpreting he told them he was sorry for their troubles. He could give them food to stop the pain of hunger, medicine for the sick and clothing for the cold, but their idea of driving the white man from the land was impossible; there were just too many of them.

Next to speak was Wandering Spirit, who leaped to his feet and began a rant, telling McLean he would die that day, and the police would all die too. He warned that the warriors would rise and go down to the fort and kill everyone. He especially singled out for killing the hated government men— the Indian Agents and farming instructors—and said they would drive the white man from the land, back to where they came from across the sea. He turned on McLean and raised his rifle to the trader's head, just as he had done to Quinn two weeks before. His heart pounding, McLean did not falter but displayed calm in the face of death. At that moment, Big Bear glided between the two and gently pushed the rifle muzzle away from McLean. The old Native scolded Wandering Spirit for acting impolitely toward their friend Straight Tongue. He spoke softly, soothing the war chief's rage until the warrior finally returned to his place in the council circle. The speeches that followed rambled on and on, and McLean began to realize he was slowly beginning to win his way in the exchange as the Crees' position softened.

Then, right in the middle of the negotiations, there was a thunder of hooves as three riders plunged through the gathering of teepees—the two NWMP constables in their red tunics and a single civilian, riding for their lives. It was Cowan, Loasby and Quinn, in a panic and trying to make it back to the fort by foolishly charging through the village at breakneck speed. McLean could only think, "Oh no—not now, not now!"

War chief Wandering Spirit, leader of the Cree forces during the Northwest Rebellion. SASKATCHEWAN ARCHIVES BOARD R-A27292

Shouts went up, "Omawhinehikew" (attackers) and "Simaganis" (police), "They will shoot us!" Thinking it was a cavalry-style attack, the warriors jumped on their horses and, in an instant, opened fire at the trio. Bent low over their saddles, the three men whipped their horses and raced onward, determined to make it to the safety of the fort on the river flat below.

David Cowan would go down first; his horse, possibly hit by a bullet, stopped running and began to buck. The young man flew from the saddle through the air, landing heavily on the ground, stunned. A Cree warrior, Louison Mongrain, pulled up and leaped off his pony to confront the prostrate Mountie before he could recover his senses. A dazed Cowan half-raised himself on one elbow and cried out, "Brother," conceding his life to his victor in surrender, as was the Cree custom. He was shot instantly. The warrior bent over and stripped off Cowan's tunic and gun belt, then slashed open the Mountie's chest and hacked out his heart. Mongrain speared it with a stick and jabbed the bloody assembly into the ground to display the extent of the policeman's bravery, which the Cree believed could be measured by the size of his heart. The constable's body would lie in that spot until Steele's Scouts came upon it nearly six weeks later.

In the meantime, Henry Quinn, less prominent in civilian dress, crashed his horse into the forest, then pulled his mount up, jumped off and slapped it onward, hiding himself in the underbrush. He escaped detection by his pursuers, eventually making his way down to the riverbank and hiding there under a tangle of exposed tree roots. The next morning, Quinn was captured. He appealed to the Cree in the same manner as Cowan had done and was allowed to live.

The third man, Clarence Loasby, continued on,

emerging from the forest in a desperate gallop for the fort with a Cree warrior right behind him, so close that their two horses jostled each other. Bullets flew all around the two, one hitting Loasby in the leg, another in the small of his back and a third probably striking his horse. The wounded mount went down in a flash as the Cree pony unavoidably slammed into it, sending the Native flying to the ground as well, only 400 metres from the fort. As the stunned Loasby lay there, the uninjured warrior jumped to his feet and scrambled toward the constable.

Amelia was the first to fire from her loophole, and Kitty quickly joined in, shooting at the menacing brave with their single-shot carbines as he hovered over the policeman, intent on stripping off his equipment before killing him. The girls' bullets zipped so closely past the Native that he retreated, leaving Loasby, still alive, lying on the ground. The girls kept up their rapid fire, driving the enemy farther and farther away and allowing the policeman time to stagger to his feet and stumble toward the fort. This also bought some time for one of the HBC clerks from the fort to sprint out and help him to safety. Loasby would live, thanks to Amelia and Kitty McLean.

During the panic, Chief Trader McLean was left under the guard of Chief Big Bear and a couple of other armed elders, making his escape impossible. Eventually, the turmoil subsided and, beyond all belief, sufficient calm was restored for negotiations to resume. To their credit,

Wandering Spirit and McLean, with Big Bear's wise coaching, would eventually reach an agreement.

McLean's deal of a lifetime was that all the civilians would become semi-volunteer hostages, meaning they would give themselves up and promise there would be no attempt by any of them to escape. For Wandering Spirit, that meant guarding the group would be far easier in the uncertain time to come. Amazingly, McLean managed to convince the war chief to allow the despised NWMP members at Fort Pitt to "conveniently" slip away that night using the newly built, leaky scow to float down the river. This freed Wandering Spirit and his braves from their traditional warrior's obligation of killing the enemy. In that way, they hoped to avoid the final consequences of massacring the whole detachment: death by hanging. Like all warriors, Wandering Spirit deeply feared this form of death for its lack of dignity.

After protecting the severely wounded Loasby through their prowess as markswomen, Amelia and Kitty McLean set aside their carbines and marched out of the fort, up the hill and brazenly into the Cree camp. As they stomped into this seething cauldron, they confronted a host of fully armed, very belligerent warriors. Amelia didn't just ask— she demanded to see their father "this instant!" Amelia was fully fluent in Cree, and because both girls appeared fearless, an attribute always admired in Cree culture, their forcefulness was tolerated. Their father saw this as an opportunity to safely communicate the terms of the agreement to the fort, so he drafted a message. The interpreter, Dufresne, translated McLean's message into Cree so Wandering Spirit and the council could understand its contents. Because McLean was to remain with the Cree as a prisoner as part of the deal, the message instructed Fort Pitt's occupants on what to do to avoid calamity in the hours to come. The girls then dutifully carried the message back to the fort and prepared for their coming term in Cree captivity.

Just after sunset, but before dark, the NWMP detachment, with the wounded Loasby strapped on the McLean's bed mattress, rushed out of the fort dragging the scow behind a team of horses. They made it the short distance to the river without incident and found the river choked with pans of ice from the spring breakup, which made their escape exceedingly dangerous. But there was no stopping now; they loaded Loasby into the flat-bottomed scow and launched it into the current, ignoring the sporadic rifle fire. The police fended off the ice as they poled and rowed their way across to the opposite side of the river. They navigated the leaky vessel around the river bend before tying up to the shore for the night and enduring a wet, swirling snow squall. It would take the contingent a wretched week to reach Fort Battleford and safety.

After the police departed, the hostages trundled out of the fort to become captives of the Cree, as agreed in the negotiations. The Cree now held 55 to 60 civilians as prisoners, many of whom were children. Once it grew dark, the Cree sacked the fort and set several of the buildings on fire.

4

Face to Face
with the Enemy

AS STRANGE AND HIS FORCE settled into their camp at the
ruined Fort Pitt, the general began making preparations
for the campaign that lay ahead. He reviewed his remaining supplies and concluded it would be necessary to put his
force on three-quarter rations. It was unclear when additional supplies would arrive, since they were coming from
Calgary in the slower-moving transport wagons. Strange
also knew that additional provisions and munitions were
coming with General Middleton on the paddlewheeled
steamboats from Fort Battleford, but Middleton's arrival
date was uncertain. To prevent pilfering, the troops were
put under threat of flogging if they were caught stealing
additional rations. However, this was a hollow threat, since

Middleton had denied Strange the authority to conduct a court martial for any disobedience. This lack of authority would plague Strange at critical times in the days to come when he was unable to mete out punishment for refusing to obey orders.

"Where is the enemy lurking?" questioned curious newspaper reporters, militia officers and soldiers alike. As conjecture grew, so did the need to determine the answer. Everyone's primary concern was saving the growing number of prisoners taken by the Cree. The newspaper reporters, especially, clamoured for immediate action, principally to create fodder for their publications. An example of the newspapers' biased reporting of the rebellion is found within the pages of the *Fort Macleod Gazette*: "Big Bear is reported to be at Sounding Lake, with four white women, who have been terribly outraged. General Strange has gone after him with blood in his eye, and it is believed and hoped will not give any quarter to these Indians, but clear them off the face of the earth."

General Strange, feeling ever-increasing pressure from the press, ordered three scouting contingents to hunt for the Cree who were holding the prisoners. Steele and his Scouts were ordered to search the area east of Onion Lake. A second group of Metis Steele's Scouts from Edmonton crossed the river and rode southwest, ultimately finding no activity, while Captain Perry, in charge of the Fort Macleod NWMP field-gun team, crossed the river and searched to the southeast. This 20-man group had orders to search toward Fort Battleford, mainly to satisfy the reporters who insisted Big Bear must have fled to the Little Pine Reserve west of Fort Battleford and joined up with Chief Poundmaker in preparation for an attack on that besieged fort. Most of the field force didn't believe that was probable; instead, Strange suspected Big Bear was somewhere in the wilderness northeast of Fort Pitt.

Steele's Scouts followed the well-used cart trail back to the northwest for about 20 kilometres, riding as far as the settlement of Onion Lake, but they turned eastward after finding no evidence of fresh Native activity. Steele led his column of Scouts along the edge of a long, crescent-shaped ridgeline that stretched east for about 15 kilometres before turning south toward the North Saskatchewan River valley.

In column formation, the weary Scouts rode into the dreary, grey evening dusk, which slowly decayed to full darkness. Rain threatened to make the night miserable, the clouds were low and the horses tired. Steele halted his column at the valley's edge overlooking the confluence of Pipestone Creek and the North Saskatchewan River. From here they could look down the river valley for miles; gazing westward, he could identify militia campfires at Fort Pitt glimmering only five kilometres away. As Steele peered down into the dark valley bottom, one of the associate Cree guides warned him, "I smell Indians." Steele took heed, but intent on a bivouac there for the night, he felt the site must be scouted out first. Because of the risk involved, he'd do it personally. He chose two of his most competent marksmen, Joe Butlin and Tom McClelland, to accompany him, while two other Scouts, Jim Oswald and William Wright, would follow discreetly a hundred metres or so behind them, acting as a rear guard in the event of an ambush. The rest of the column remained at the top of the valley while Steele and his group descended the steep trail to the valley floor to conduct their reconnaissance of the creek.

The riders followed along the bank of the Pipestone Creek, riding as far as the North Saskatchewan River. The trio warily surveyed their surroundings in the midnight darkness as their weary horses silently covered the soft, damp ground. Steele scrutinized the shadowy setting as the horses waded across the shallow confluence of creek and river. They swung around and began their return along the opposite bank toward the main column of Scouts. Steele spoke to his companions in a low tone, "Perfect place for us to bivouac for a few hours; our horses and the men need a rest."

Suddenly, from just metres in front of Steele's horse, a brilliant flash of orange and red flame stabbed toward him, accompanied by a horrendous bang. A bullet zinged past, snipping at the cuff of his scarlet tunic, and his mount, despite its training, shied and danced sideways, threatening to buck. An ambush! Steele held the startled animal in check with one hand and groped his revolver from its holster with the other.

The Cree warrior Meminook had missed killing Steele. In an instant, Meminook leaped up from concealment and dashed in front of Steele to his own horse in a race to escape. Diving across his mount's bare back, Meminook flung a leg over to bring himself into a sitting position, just as Joe Butlin fired his Winchester. Butlin's bullet was true to its mark, striking the warrior in the throat and killing him instantly; the lifeless body tumbled to the ground with a soft thump.

A second flash of fire erupted from another warrior's rifle just as Steele spotted him crouched under a tree. The bullet zinged past Sam, who snapped a return shot with his pistol but also missed. Other muzzle flashes erupted out of the dark, coming from all directions, like a swarm of bees searching out the trio. The desperate Scouts, dismounted and standing their ground, returned fire as fast as they could lever new cartridges into their Winchesters. Swearing and shouting warnings, the Scouts frantically fired and reloaded, again and again. All of the combatants were blinded by the brilliant muzzle flashes and frantically fought on in the dark, not knowing if they were having any effect on the enemy. The Cree, now mounted, seemed to be everywhere, and the three Scouts were clearly in trouble. The fight had happened so quickly that their trailing rear guard had no time to charge to their aid as planned. It seemed the fight went on for an eternity. Where were the others?

This 1885 sketch by General Strange captures the moment when Sam Steele and two of his Scouts stumbled into a gunfight at midnight with the Cree at Pipestone Creek. GLENBOW ARCHIVES NA-1817-4

The flashes of fire suddenly ceased, leaving the Scouts standing with rifles ready in the dark as the pounding of hooves faded off to the east. For a moment there was only the rapid, heavy breathing of the three men. "Holy . . . that was wild!" said one. Suddenly Oswald and Wright charged up out of the dark, reining up in front of the trio, too late to help.

The next day, one of the American supply-wagon drivers scalped Meminook's dead body, then looped a lasso around the Native's neck and dragged the corpse behind his saddle horse in huge circles around the river flat. The warrior's scalp would hang for years in a Calgary pool hall as an unrecognizable, morbid trophy. Meminook's desecrated body was never buried, and General Strange recalls seeing the bloated form lying not far from the creek days later. It was a sad, disgusting end for a highly respected headman from the Saddle Lake Reserve. He'd joined the rebellion believing it was the only way to better the lives of his destitute family. Oddly, just before Meminook rode out of the Cree camp earlier that evening, he'd shared a premonition of his demise with William Cameron, a survivor of the Frog Lake massacre and a prisoner, who later told his story in his book *Blood Red the Sun:*

> The night we camped in the coulee I saw Meeminook [*sic*], his face smeared with vermilion and yellow ochre, leave his lodge buckling on his cartridge belt. I asked where he was going—the reason for the paint.
>
> "To the fort." He stood looking down at me with his engaging friendly smile, his fine eyes dancing, took my hand and pressed it. "If I do not come back—well, what of it? It is what comes to us all some time. Remember always, Meeminook was your friend!"

Over at Fort Pitt, sitting at his portable desk reading scouting reports, General Strange was wide-eyed at hearing gunfire coming from such a short distance away. He burst from his tent and bellowed, "Bugler, sound assembly!" He needn't have bothered. Every man in the camp had heard the rattle of gunfire and was frantically pulling on his boots and strapping on equipment as fast as he could. Strange ordered the 65th Mount Royal Rifles back to their scows on the river while the 92nd Winnipeg Light Infantry—197 of them—were loaded into wagons to be quickly transported down the trail toward the skirmish. Most of the supplies were still loaded on other wagons that only needed to be hitched up. Assembly took just a few minutes. The nine-pound NWMP field gun was another matter, as the trained gun team was with Captain Perry, now under General Middleton's thumb and sitting in utter frustration in Fort Battleford. The only man in the Alberta Field Force who knew anything about artillery was Strange's son, Harry, who took command of the field piece and commandeered a half-dozen Winnipeg Light Infantry volunteers. This inexperienced group hooked up the horses to the field gun and caisson in time to join the quickly departing procession as it moved out into the grey, overcast dawn.

Strange's column took only about an hour to cover the short distance to Pipestone Creek, finding Steele and his Scouts deployed in a defensive position behind trees and rocks along the creek bank, Winchesters at the ready. Since the attack, it had been deathly quiet as a chilling light drizzle of rain fell. No one slept and the tired horses were without food; even so, it was soon time to mount up. The Scouts, as usual, led the way eastward along the river-flat trail parallel to the North Saskatchewan. Steele ordered John Whitford, a Metis from Edmonton, to lead six Scouts ahead of the main column, and in a short time they became engulfed in thick underbrush along the riverbank, losing contact with each other. Whitford heard some rustling in the foliage but could only see part of a buckskin-clad leg and the flank of a horse through a small gap in the willows. To determine who was there, he attempted a ruse. In a low tone he queried in Cree, "Shall we fight, or fall back?"

The reply came in Cree, "Let us draw them, to fight is no good. We were not sent here for that."

As soon as he heard Cree spoken in response, Whitford spurred his horse and charged ahead through the brush, shouting to his companions, "Ride for it boys, Indians!" The race was on as they dashed for their lives, galloping back to the protection of the main column as fast as the horses would go, with a whooping, yipping war party of Cree close behind.

Steele, at the head of his column, spotted his men racing toward them, the yelling warriors close behind. He shouted, "Dismount! Prepare for attack!" and the column of Scouts leaped from their mounts, pulled the horses down onto the ground and prepared to open fire on command. Whitford and his boys charged through the defensive perimeter to safety while the war party reined in, turned and retreated without firing a shot. Once the dust had settled, Whitford told Steele how he'd identified who was in the bush. He was met with a hearty laugh from his commander, and the stunt became the highlight of the morning as it was relayed back through the ranks.

The column formed up again and moved four kilometres east along the river flats to Oldman Creek. Here the trail made a turn to the left, following up the ravine to finally break into the open at the base of a ridge that forms a step in the land running north to south. On the crest of this prominence, many of the soldiers saw their enemy for the first time. Cree warriors, silhouetted against a clear blue sky, raced their ponies around and waved their rifles. They whooped and yipped, daring the militia to attack. Years later, many of the 1885 veterans would still recall this vivid scene as they related their experiences to avid listeners.

Instead of attacking, General Strange ordered up the field gun. Harry Strange instructed his new gun team on the procedure of loading the field piece as they prepared to fire. Discharging this weapon was a tedious process; the pre-measured powder charge was placed in the muzzle and rammed home to the barrel's base with a ramrod, then the explosive charge primer hole of the shell was pierced before the shell was placed into the barrel and rammed home on top of the powder charge. Next, the friction tube primer, which is cross-shaped and about the size of a ballpoint pen, was inserted vertically in its hole at the base of the barrel and a firing lanyard was attached to the removable horizontal friction pin's D ring. The gun was then sighted and elevated for the approximate distance to the target. The crew were now ready to fire.

Harry Strange bellowed the order, "Ready—Fiah!" The gunner gave a fast, strong, steady pull on the lanyard that drew the friction pin quickly out of the tube, creating the heat needed to ignite the primer's charge. With a chest-compressing, heart-stopping boom, the piece went off, sending the gun carriage reeling backward from the recoil. The shell travelled 600 metres in a half second, exploding with a second huge bang. (The Cree consequently dubbed it, "The gun that speaks twice.") The whole process was then repeated, except this time the barrel was hot, and the crew had to first quench the residual burning gunpowder with water. The barrel was washed out and swabbed dry before they began loading again. The process proved horrendously slow for Harry's untrained team and provided the Cree with a significant amount of time—as much as two minutes—to safely move about after the shell struck. After a second shot was fired, there wasn't a warrior to be seen. The Cree were now aware they were facing something new and dangerous. Jingo Strange confidently ordered a ceasefire; he'd sent the clear message that he and his militia were there on serious business.

Meanwhile, the 65th Mount Royal Rifles, apprehensively riding in their scows, had drifted with the current to the confluence of Little Red Deer River and the North Saskatchewan River, about two kilometres south of today's

Deer Creek Bridge on the North Saskatchewan. Hearing the boom of the field gun, they put in to shore, just at mealtime. Ignoring their hot dinners, they excitedly jumped from their vessels and quickly assembled into marching order. Colonel Hughes, their commander, marched them up the creek valley to the Carlton Trail's ford, then followed the trail west in the hopes of pinching the enemy between themselves and Strange's force and committing the Cree to battle.

With the disappearance of the warriors off the ridge, Strange ordered his men into skirmish order. Because of their repeating Winchesters, the Scouts led the troops, well spread out, up the barren slope. They reached the crest without opposition, only to be confronted with a forest of young poplar trees, their trunks 5 to 10 centimetres thick. Steele noted in his autobiography that "the trees had infested the country significantly since the first time I was through," which was with Inspector Jarvis's column during the NWMP Great March West of 1874. The Scouts and infantry cautiously advanced in skirmish order through the trees, taking extreme care with each step. Occasionally a shot rang out when one of them thought they saw a target, but no confrontations occurred.

It took most of the day to advance only five kilometres along the Carlton Trail to the base of a high, dome-like prominence known as Frenchman Butte, where they met up with Colonel Hughes' force. In an open area at the base of the west side of the hill, they discovered a newly constructed Cree sun-dance lodge with signs of very recent use. The lodge, made of poplar trees with the leaves left on the branches, looked like a gigantic teepee, except a large tree held up the center of the structure. Near the roof hung a ball made of entwined willow branches with large ribbons or streamers of coloured cloth attached. The sun dance was a ritual performed by young men wishing to advance to warrior status. To accomplish that, they were expected to prove themselves by piercing their chest muscles with sharp bones or stakes attached to long thongs of buffalo hide or rope that were fixed to the top of the pole. The warriors danced around the pole, throwing themselves backward against the taunt thongs until the bones or wooden spears tore through the muscle tissue and freed them.

The enemy was close, but it was now sundown and time to bivouac for the night. Doubled guards were set, and Scouts ranged out on patrol as the wagons were circled. As he took stock of the situation, General Strange realized that his force had little food, few blankets and limited field-gun ammunition. Both sections of his force had departed in such an excited rush that little thought had been given to such necessities. To ease the situation, the force pooled what little food they had, mainly hardtack biscuits that individual soldiers had stuffed in their "possibles bag," an early version of the kit bag common to all armies. There was at least hot tea at suppertime, but the warming fires were extinguished with the coming of night. General Strange ordered the wagons into a tight circle with the horses on the inside, and the soldiers crawled under the wagons to attempt some sleep on the cold, damp ground, sharing the few blankets among them. Strange ordered the soldiers not to fire their rifles during the night, as in the dark they risked shooting one of their own, especially since Steele and the Scouts were patrolling the camp's outside perimeter on horseback. The entire force sensed the enemy was close, and most soldiers got only a few short hours of sleep as they lay on the ground pondering the coming day and what it would bring.

5

The Battle Is Joined

ON MAY 28, AT THE break of daylight, the men were quietly rousted without the benefit of the traditional reveille bugle call. Stiff, sore and famished, they shuffled into skirmish order so the advance could begin once again. The morning fog shrouded the young poplar trees, creating a ghostly setting and limiting their view of any potential enemy. The force moved cautiously forward, working their way parallel to a freshly travelled spur of the Carlton Trail. At about 6 AM, they came upon what is now called Stand-off Coulee, a tributary valley of the Little Red Deer River (renamed the Monnery River when the country was surveyed). As the fog began to lift with the warming air, it promised to be a beautiful sunny, windless day.

With rifles at the ready, the point Scouts cautiously moved along the trail northward until they came to the edge of a deep ravine where the trail they were following descended down the slope to the valley floor. Beside the trail where they had halted, a dying campfire smouldered; on its coals a fresh bannock cake still baked. Steele was summoned to examine the site and ordered two of his Scouts—the experienced NWMP sergeant William Parker and a civilian, Alex Rowland, from Edmonton—to reconnoitre the valley floor. The two men urged their horses forward and plunged down the steep incline to the valley bottom. There they discovered a sodden, swampy morass, and when they tried to cross, Rowland's horse immediately became mired in the ooze, sinking to its withers. Snorting and thrashing, it eventually plunged back to solid ground. The pair of Scouts quickly concluded that with the corduroy swamp crossing recently torn out, continuing on would be exceedingly difficult,

As both men looked up toward the opposite ridge, the hair on their necks stood up. Sensing imminent danger, they turned and casually made their way back up the slope. On reaching the top again, the two relieved Scouts reported to Steele what they'd discovered in their foray and the danger that they sensed lay beyond.

During the time the two Scouts were in the valley, Steele and Strange had studied the opposite side of the ravine with binoculars. Peering across the valley through the quickly dwindling fog patches, they had identified freshly dug earth and tree branches covering what appeared to be fortifications along the valley's crest. In contrast, far to their right, bright red cloth streamers hung high in the trees, motionless in the calm of the morning but beckoning their attention—all indications of a trap.

The night before, on the Cree side of the valley, many of the non-combatant Natives—the old, and the women and children—and over 50 prisoners had been directed by Wandering Spirit to dig their own protective dugouts well behind the main defensive warrior rifle pits on the crest of the valley. These dugouts were situated along a shallow ravine where an old, little used cart trail ascended. The farming instructor from Onion Lake, George Mann, later wrote that he chose to dig his family's dugout into the slope of the ravine a few metres from the McLeans' refuge. The McLean bunker was large enough for all 10 family members. Because there were few tools available, most of the dugouts were relatively shallow, only about a metre deep. The prisoners heaped the earth from the hole around its perimeter, and some occupants also added logs and branches across the top to provide overhead protection as well. In total, about 70 non-combatant refuge dugouts were dug away from the firing line.

Many of the Native women and children didn't remain at the battle site but travelled north another six kilometres that evening to establish a second camp in a protected, semi-hidden valley. It was intended that this more-distant camp would serve as an interim sanctuary for them and the wounded as the battle progressed. They also dug a number of rifle pits near the valley's entrance for use in defence of the camp should the soldiers follow up with an immediate attack. A ridgetop lookout position offered an unobstructed view all the way back to Frenchman Butte, enabling lookouts to give the camp sufficient warning to evacuate if the militia pursued them.

On the battle line, warriors dug their rifle pits facing south and west, just back from the ravine's crest. This positioning provided reasonable protection, and since many of the warriors still fired old muzzleloading rifles, they needed a safe place to conduct the complex process of reloading. Once their rifles were reloaded, they would crawl on their bellies out of the pits and up to the crest of the hill, choose a target in the valley below and fire, then scramble back to their pits to reload again.

General Strange decided to confirm the presence of a Cree trap and ordered up the gun team. Harry and his volunteers galloped up in a rush, dismounted and prepared the field gun for firing. With the general's approval, Harry yelled, "Ready—fiah!" The gunner gave a strong pull on the lanyard and set off the artillery piece, which jumped back as it sent a shell whistling toward the opposite side of the valley. Following the practice of "ranging in," he'd first aimed high, then fired the next shot low; as the gap narrowed, Harry's shells zeroed in on the target.

On the opposite side the valley, the Native defenders awoke at dawn, after spending the night curled up in their damp dugout fortifications. Chief Big Bear visited the non-combatant Natives and white prisoners at their dugouts. He warned everybody of the great danger posed by "the gun that speaks twice" and told them that they wouldn't be safe, even in their dugout sanctuaries. He advised they leave immediately and walk to the north, spreading out to avoid leaving an identifiable trail as they made their way to the second camp. The McLean family, along with the other hostages, took his advice and began their trek northward. The hostages involuntarily ducked when the first artillery shell flew overhead, followed by a final bang as the shell exploded far ahead. The white hostages realized they were close to being rescued, while the Native women and children were scared of the strange new weapon, yet all were forced to press on.

When the second shell hit, many of the jittery Cree warriors in the rifle pits opened fire on the field gun's smoke, revealing their positions and their intent to stand their ground. General Strange immediately ordered his infantry and Scouts to line up from west to east. The dismounted Steele's Scouts were on the western flank, then the 65th Mount Royal Rifles and the 92nd Winnipeg Light Infantry; on the far eastern flank were Major George Hatton and his Alberta Mounted Rifles Cavalry, also dismounted. About 175 metres to the rear, Strange situated his supply wagons and two disappointed companies of the Winnipeg Light Infantry, who were held in reserve and would not see combat. Ammunition runners would carry additional rounds from the supply wagons, which were circled at the rear to replenish the soldiers on the firing line. Spillage was common during the battle, and the wastage appeared to be significant as the runners hurried about their duty of transporting ammunition to the front line. The paths they took from the wagons to the soldiers became strewn with unspent cartridges as the battle progressed.

The bugler sounded "advance," and the line of militia and scouts moved forward, scrambling down the steep hillside and moving from tree to tree, firing as they went. As the soldiers reached the bottom of the slope, they came upon the debilitating swamp that Parker and Whitford had discovered earlier. There was no choice but to take cover as best they could, lying behind protective trees, an occasional rock and clumps of willow. Sprawling on their bellies, they began firing at the puffs of gunsmoke coming from Native rifles aimed down on them. The soldiers faced a serious dilemma. They were poorly protected where they were, yet it was impossible to advance into the swamp and dangerous to retreat since they would be highly exposed going back up the hill.

Donald McRae, an NWMP trooper and Scout, was lying behind a willow clump and took a bullet in his left thigh early in the battle. His buddies crawled through the flying bullets to his aid, but he pleaded for them just to put a bandage on the wound for the time being; he wanted to finish off his allotment of ammunition "on those damn redskins." Both Steele and Strange, recognizing his pluck and determination and considering the low-risk location of the wound, granted him permission, saying, "Carry on, trooper." McRae's exact location was determined decades later after the discovery of a single concentration of expended 45-75 cartridge casings.

Harry Strange and the field-gun crew soon discovered their field of fire had failed to include all of the Cree positions. Some of the Cree rifle pits were north of the elbow of the ravine and could not be reached from their location. Harry requested permission to withdraw the field piece and reposition it about 500 metres to the west, opposite the point of the valley's elbow. This new position would allow the field gun to fire on the positions on both sides of the bend from one position. After the field gun was relocated, it became far more effective. Harry initially loaded air-burst shells containing steel-ball shrapnel for the initial ranging shots that he could observe, but he soon discovered the delayed-fuse style of shell was more effective, since it would lie momentarily dormant in the ground where it struck before exploding.

The field gun initially posed a frightening problem for the Cree, but once the battle commenced, many of them quickly discovered its slow rate of fire and took advantage of the lag. One warrior routinely jumped up into full view each time a shell landed, waving and shouting at the troops, "Tan-at-ee! Tan-at-ee!" Apparently, he had spent some time around the NWMP posts and observed the reaction of the men when the command "Stand at ease!" was ordered. Not understanding that the command applied to a parade-square environment, he thought it might encourage the gunners to relax or lay off.

One significant incident illustrates the havoc caused by the field gun. It happened in a rifle pit prominently situated on the north end of the Cree defences. The pit faced west and was situated around the crook of the valley's elbow, not far from today's district road. About three or four metres long and well over a metre wide, the pit housed a number of warriors. This particular fortification took a direct hit from the militia's field gun shortly after Harry repositioned it. Harry's volunteer gunner was able to fire two shells close to the pit and finally landed a shell inside it, mortally wounding a Cree warrior, Kahwechatwaymat, cutting his leg artery with shrapnel. Unable to stem the bleeding, he died late in the day and was buried a short distance north of the fortification. The exact location of his grave is unknown. Kahwechatwaymat is the only known fatality in the battle; the number of wounded on the Native side is unknown since there are no written Native accounts of the battle. Only oral history remains, and it is silent on such details.

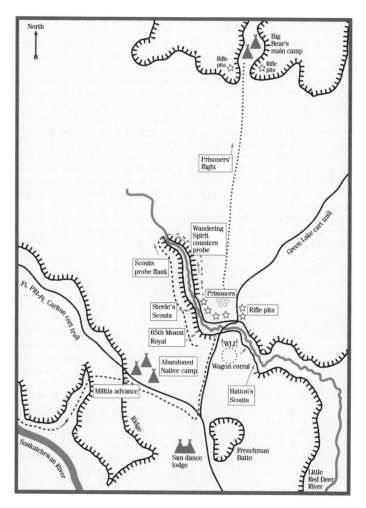

The positions of General Strange's forces and the Cree during the Battle of Frenchman Butte. TOM HOWELL

Throughout the battle, the gun team was exposed to a sharpshooting Metis buffalo hunter turned sniper extraordinaire, Weekwaypan (Trousers), who constantly picked at them with his Sharps buffalo rifle. His aim proved so accurate that he regularly pinged slugs off the field gun's barrel. In response, General Strange ordered the vulnerable gun team to reload their artillery piece in a safer manner, on their knees.

The Cree defences held up well, and as the battle stalled, the prospect of a military success dwindled by the hour. Strange ordered Steele's Scouts to withdraw and remount their horses to conduct a reconnaissance in force along the valley's edge to the northwest, attempting to find a point on that flank where the force could successfully cross on foot and attack. Meanwhile, the infantry spread out to fill the vacated Scout positions.

After Steele and his Scouts mounted up in column order, they rode northwestward along the valley for three or four kilometres. A vigilant Wandering Spirit, the Cree war chief, was on the opposite side of the valley and spotted the Scouts' manoeuvre. With three or four other warriors, he ran through the underbrush paralleling Steele's course. Sporadically, the astute Cree would pause, open fire on the Scouts and then run on, giving Steele the impression that the Cree fortifications occupied the entire valley, extending almost indefinitely. At one point, Sergeant William Parker requested permission from Steele to climb a huge spruce tree to gain a view of the country across the valley. From this risky and very sticky vantage point, Parker saw many Natives abandoning the battlefield and fleeing northward—this proved to be the stream of non-combatants. The Scouts also found a portion of the creek where the valley flattened out, which would allow a crossing in force. Having accomplished their task, Steele and the Scouts returned to the battle and reported to General Strange.

But in addition to Steele's encouraging report, Strange was receiving news, later proved erroneous, that the supply wagons were coming under fire from Cree snipers in the woods to his rear. Believing the reports to be true, he ordered Hatton's dismounted cavalry to adjust their defences and extend their eastern perimeter to give the teamsters time to move the wagons to a safer but more distant location. Strange also received a report from the Mount Royal Rifles that two infantrymen, Private Joseph LeMai and Private Joseph Marcotte, had been wounded on the firing line below. LeMai, the most seriously wounded of the two, was shot in the left lung and left to die there by his commanders. Marcotte had sustained a lesser wound in the chest, but his regimental buddies were able to evacuate him from his vulnerable forward position. An angry, indignant Strange demanded that the remaining soldier be rescued, but the sullen reply from the wounded man's officer was, "General, I have been shot at enough for one day and I am damned if I'll go down there again!" The officer then turned his back on Strange and stomped away. Strange, unable to prosecute the officer in a court martial, could do nothing but summon up a couple of volunteer stretcher bearers and, with the regiment's chaplain, Father Paré, go to the bottom of the ravine to retrieve the wounded man himself. In short order, this small rescue party scrambled to the valley bottom amid a storm of ball and bullets and succeeded in locating the still-conscious private. Father Paré began to administer last rites as the wounded man was carefully loaded onto the stretcher by the stretcher bearers. With bullets continually zinging past their ears, Strange suggested the praying chaplain "rush it a little." Climbing the valley slope with the wounded soldier was difficult for the stretcher bearers, and on the way up the steep incline, one of them dropped his end of the stretcher as he struggled along. The general, without hesitation, jumped in to help carry the wounded LeMai up over the brink of the valley to safety and an eventual full recovery.

It was now decision time. General Strange was faced with a number of troubling factors and decided the wisest action was to withdraw from the battle in an orderly fashion. Attack was not feasible. Although Steele had reported a possible avenue existed on the left flank, with limited numbers of battle-weary troops and the Cree strongly entrenched on the opposite side, a frontal attack up a barren slope would be suicidal. In addition, they were beginning to run low on ammunition, and some of Strange's commanders were becoming increasingly insubordinate in their attitude as the reality of being in actual combat had set in. Most alarming, though, were the unconfirmed reports of snipers in the rear firing on the wagons. Strange feared that like Custer's soldiers, they would become surrounded.

Steele and his Scouts were the last to leave the battle-field, acting as a rearguard to the main force while they moved out. The evacuation began at about 2 PM in the afternoon, eight hours after the battle's commencement. It marked the end of the last official battle fought in Canada by Canadian troops.

The members of the 65th Mount Royal Rifles, under Colonel Hughes, were in for some serious marching once they withdrew from the firing line. Initially, they formed up into their ranks and retraced their march of the day before, back down the Carlton Trail to the Little Red Deer (Monnery) River, then turned downstream, following along the top of the valley to where the scows had been left tied up on the North Saskatchewan River.

On arrival at the river, Hughes was dismayed to discover that the jumpy boat crews had panicked and cast off upon hearing gunfire seemingly coming from every direction as it echoed in the early morning fog. The flotilla had drifted downstream on the current about two kilometres and hidden behind an island to await the outcome of the fight-ing. On discovering the scows were gone, Colonel Hughes had no choice but to turn his men around and grudgingly march back to rejoin General Strange and the rest of the Alberta Field Force. As the reunited force, exhausted and discouraged, shuffled back to Fort Pitt, Strange dispatched a messenger to the fort telling the cooks to get the fires going and prepare a good meal for the men. When they marched into camp late that night, the soldiers were immediately dismissed to dispose of their rifles in a traditional muzzle-together haystack in front of their shelters. Then they rushed and jostled to line up for their first real grub in two terribly long days. With their stomachs warmed and full, the thoroughly disillusioned troops headed to their bedrolls for what was left of the night.

6

In Pursuit of Big Bear

BACK IN FORT PITT, GENERAL STRANGE stewed over General Middleton's communications. Nearly all of them contained details that seemed at odds with Steele's scouting reports. Many messages included erroneous information and conflicting orders. Forthcoming supplies, troops and arms, even his errant scouting party under Inspector Bowen-Perry seemed to be lost and "elsewhere" than indicated in Middleton's messages. In one case, a paddle-wheeled steamboat supposedly loaded with desperately needed supplies turned out to be carrying more nosy, arrogant reporters than goods when it arrived at the Fort Pitt landing.

In his memoirs, Strange laments that his messengers

were like "ravens sent out from the Ark—they never seemed to come back." Finally, to Strange's relief, Captain Dudley-Smith showed up late on May 29 with a convoy of supply wagons from Edmonton, easing the supply shortage.

To his frustration, Strange also learned that the Metis scouts detailed to keep the Cree under surveillance had lost track of the Cree warriors after they had fled from the coulee battle site. The location of the main body of Natives was, once again, uncertain.

After only one day's rest, Strange reassembled the force. Despite being lightly outfitted, they marched out of Fort Pitt back to Frenchman Butte. Here they re-established their previous camp, cramming themselves into the few tents they'd brought with them. The next morning, Sunday, May 31, reveille was sounded in heavy rain, and when the slicker-suited Scouts came in, they reported seeing individual Cree warriors prowling about nearly everywhere they patrolled. The Natives were also spotted at the battle site, rummaging through the abandoned wagons that had once been loaded with supplies from the previously plundered Fort Pitt.

A significant change was occurring within the Native ranks, signalling the disintegration of their fragile alliance. After the Frog Lake incident on April 2, the Native bands in the region had united into one large group; fearing the Queen's soldiers, they sought safety in numbers. Many of the leaders responsible for initiating the murders were Plains Cree, such as Wandering Spirit, Little Poplar, Imassees and others. While their brothers, the Woods Cree, supported them, they were reluctant to become militantly aggressive, other than to protect themselves. A third group, the Chipewyan, were of the Dene Nation and came from the Cold Lake area. The Chipewyan were highly influenced by their priest, Father Le Goff, who cautioned strongly against warfare. Their involvement in hostilities was very limited, as they feared severe military retribution when the hostilities ended.

The combined three groups initially numbered about 1,300 individuals; however, only an estimated 300 were actually front-line fighters. After the Battle of Frenchman Butte, the Chipewyan became very uncomfortable about the Plains Cree–dominated relationship and deliberately began lagging behind the fleeing main group. The opportunity to escape the relationship presented itself with the dense morning fog on the day of the battle. After freeing the hostages they had been assigned to guard, they slipped away into the wilderness, heading toward their abandoned reserve community at Le Goff, located south of Cold Lake. The trading post of Beaver Crossing was along the route, and they intended to stop there for supplies.

The dozen hostages freed by the Chipewyan wandered on their own in the Perch Lake country east of the battle site for three days, hiding in fear of being recaptured by the Cree. They eventually climbed Frenchman Butte for a vantage point. During the evening of May 31, they intercepted Sergeant William Parker and his party of Scouts as they rode along the Carlton Trail, which bent around the southern base of the hill. Parker immediately brought them to Steele at the Scouts' main camp. One of them, the sole male white survivor of the Frog Lake massacre, William Cameron, gave Steele valuable information on the condition of the remaining captives and the direction they were travelling. Steele immediately dispatched a message to Strange, who responded with an order for Steele to take "a flying column of scouts" and pursue the Cree to the fullest. After his force had failed to free the prisoners during the battle, Strange knew there was an increasing risk that the Cree might murder them all before evaporating into the wilderness. A sudden attack conducted at the earliest opportunity would catch the enemy by surprise. He hoped the captives would be left unattended and thus be rescued in the ensuing confusion.

On reading Strange's orders at 2:00 AM on June 1, Steele leaped onto his horse and galloped through the camp, bellowing "Get up, men. Get up! Get eight days half rations and follow me!" He then charged off down the trail, heading northward. Pandemonium erupted in the camp; 75 men scrambled from their beds, hurriedly pulled on their boots and grabbed whatever they needed, including cans of bully beef (corned beef), hardtack biscuits and ammunition, stuffing everything into bulging saddlebags. As fast as they could saddle the horses, the Scouts mounted up and rode after their commander, forming up into their regular positions as they went and eventually catching up to Steele.

The column rode northward about six kilometres, warily following a small creek to enter an almost hidden valley. Here they found the abandoned second camp of the Cree with a few teepees, more forsaken wagons, carts loaded with bales of fur and discarded supplies strewn everywhere. They also eyed the excavated defensive rifle pits dug along the valley entrance—deadly traps had they been manned by the warriors. From this camp, tracks led to the northwest, and Steele discovered a pencilled note written by William McLean pinned to a branch along the trail. McLean wrote that all prisoners were well and to look for them to the northwest. That valuable information provided the Scouts with some sense of direction as they pressed on.

The Cree were doing everything in their power to hinder anyone following them. They felled huge trees, set bush fires, tore up the corduroy that covered boggy areas, and laid false trails across swampy muskegs to dead ends. The trail was exceedingly difficult for the horses, while the Scouts were taxed to the limit and poorly prepared for their foray. In the rush to get away from camp, they hadn't even brought an axe. Mosquitos swarmed them at night, and bulldogs and deer flies chewed on them during the day, harassing the exasperated men and horses alike, nearly driving them mad. Some of the horses even stood in the smouldering smudges meant to protect them.

Steele told his Scouts, "I wait for no one; if you or your horse is injured and goes down, it's up to you to make your way back down the trail to camp. You're on your own; is that understood?" Half a can of bully beef and a hardtack biscuit was the ration per meal. There was no hay for the horses; when there was time, they grazed on meadow grasses, which had few nutrients, and both horses and men drank swamp or lake water. Consequently, by the time they reached Loon Lake the next day, there were only enough horses left for 47 of the approximately 63 Scouts.

From the valley camp, the trail meandered northwest another eight kilometres to a camp described in several journals as "located in a park-like setting" on the shore of Horse Lake (now Sidney Lake). Here the Cree paused and recuperated from the battle for a couple of days before beginning their flight through the wilderness toward Loon Lake. The remaining white prisoners were still under light guard and endured the challenges they faced with each kilometre they hiked, fearing they would be shot if they fell behind. They trudged on in the company of the Cree non-combatants, including elderly men, women and children, who were motivated by their own fear of the soldiers who they expected would be hot on their heels. As they trekked north, the food supply dwindled and the warriors did their best to supplement the few supplies available by hunting rabbits, small animals and birds as they went. William McLean was trusted enough by the Cree to be allowed a muzzleloader and hunted with them for wild game.

In Pursuit of Big Bear

The McLeans, along with fellow prisoners Theresa Gowanlock and Theresa Delaney, survivors from Frog Lake, wrote in their memoirs of the hardships encountered on their trek. They waded creeks where the water almost came to their armpits; their shredded clothing hung on them like rags, and they slept at night in rain-sodden blankets or with no blankets at all. The women were also exposed to the constant threat of sexual assault by the young Cree men. Louison Mongrain, the warrior who had killed Constable Cowan at Fort Pitt, played a significant role in protecting them from harm. All of the adult prisoners took turns carrying the young children for hours on end, struggling up hills and down, constantly stumbling through the bush in weariness.

Continuing on the trail from Horse Lake as it rambled northward along the west side of the Little Red Deer River, the Scouts finally came to an open, grassy meadow. It appeared to be an ideal place to take a noon break and let the horses graze for a few minutes. The Scouts' chaplain, the well-armed George McKay, and another Calgary Scout, Jim "Jumbo" Fisk, unnoticed by Steele, went on ahead to the opposite side of the lush, expansive clearing. A few metres inside the treeline, the preacher spotted a Cree warrior walking toward him through the trees, using the same trail. McKay levelled his Winchester at the man and waited. The warrior was just a few metres away from McKay when the minister squeezed the trigger, sending a bullet singing past the man's ear. The Native dropped instantly as if he were dead, then bounded up, turned and dashed off into the surrounding forest. Fisk, still mounted, came galloping up to help, and another unseen Native lurking in the brush fired at Fisk, hitting him in the wrist, the bullet exiting the Scout's elbow and nearly knocking him from his horse.

Hearing the shooting, Steele and the rest of the Scouts jumped up and charged across the meadow toward Fisk and McKay. Steele described McKay's appearance and actions in his journal; he found him "dressed in a pea jacket, felt hat, moccasins and having tied up his pants with thongs at both the knee and ankle, running wildly through the underbrush, yelling, yipping and hollering, uttering the best of an Indian style war cry." The warriors had vanished, and despite the Scouts' best effort, the abrupt little skirmish ended in disappointment. The bones in Jim Fisk's arm had been splintered, and he endured this painful wound for three more days without medical aid. The injury would handicap him for the rest of his life.

Later, Steele asked McKay why he missed hitting his target at such close range. McKay refused to admit that he had, with a clear shot, deliberately missed his mark, but mumbled sheepishly in explanation, "I am a man of God after all, and besides, why kill a man when you can frighten him into doing your bidding?"

Steele led his men on, aware that other Cree warriors could be lying in ambush, trying to stop his column from catching up to their fleeing people. Finally, at about midnight, Steele called a halt at a place he indicates in his journal was between two small lakes. The weary Scouts, having ridden for over 20 hours, unsaddled their horses and quickly built a barricade from logs and saddles. Steele assigned two Scouts to guard duty so the rest could eat some of their rations and catch a few hours of sleep.

There are few identifying details of the actual route followed by the Cree and the pursuing Scouts between Horse Lake and Loon Lake. Historical survey maps of the early 1900s, along with scarce journal comments, suggest that both forces travelled northwards, parallel to the Little Red Deer River, part way to Little Fishing Lake before crossing this drainage to continue through extremely challenging terrain around the east side of Little Fishing Lake. Once north of that lake, their trail followed higher ground on the east side of a lengthy muskeg, then turned northward at a point just north of Goose Lake to approach Sanderson Bay on Loon Lake from the south. Maps from the 1920s agree with pioneer accounts that identify this route as the Red Cross–Loon Lake Trail.

Two days after the Battle of Frenchman Butte, General Middleton had arrived with his force on a sternwheeled riverboat and established his camp on a river flat four kilometres east of Fort Pitt. Here he prepared to head northeast into the wilderness to follow Steele and his Scouts, who were now closing in on the fleeing Cree. Realizing the difficulty of the terrain that lay ahead, Middleton abandoned the idea

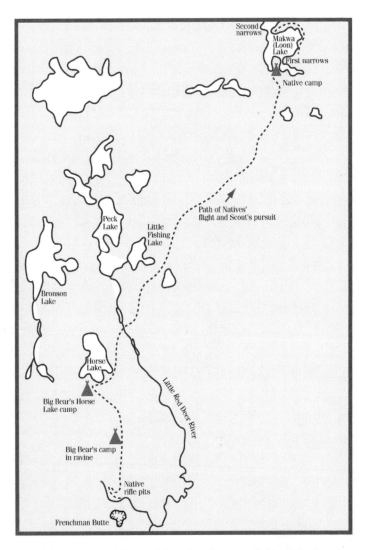

The likely route followed by the Cree and Steele's Scouts
following the Battle of Frenchman Butte. TOM HOWELL

of marching his full force and instead organized a compact mounted contingent using pack horses to carry supplies and ammunition. It took a day to construct cargo frames for the horses so he moved his camp about five kilometres to the ridge on the Carlton Trail where Harry Strange had first fired the field gun at the mounted warriors. Middleton also decided to bring the lighter Gatling guns, rather than struggle with the heavy field gun. On June 1, his mounted force finally set out from the camp to follow up on Steele's trail.

As the Scouts moved north, Steele sent Joe Butlin, leading an advanced patrol, to scout the route ahead. In the dark, Butlin followed the clearly visible Cree track that continued northeastward a short distance from their bivouac before turning straight north. Arriving at a point of land overlooking Loon Lake, Butlin looked down on a small cluster of teepees a half-kilometre away, nestled in a lush basin surrounded by hills to the north and west and the sparkling blue water of Loon Lake to the east. Butlin sent a messenger back to Steele advising him he was in sight of their enemy, then settled down to wait near a large rock.

7

The Loon Lake Melee

SHORTLY AFTER 9:00 AM on June 3, Sam Steele, at the head
of his column of Scouts, rode up to Joe Butlin's vantage point
overlooking the iridescent blue bay. The light morning breeze
created tiny wavelets that sparkled like diamonds on the
water in the brilliant sunshine. Even Steele paused momentarily to appreciate the picturesque setting; he later remarked
upon it in his autobiography, *Forty Years in Canada*: "Before
us lay a large and very beautiful lake with many pretty bays; a
long point jutted out from the east side of it, and might be an
island; it was densely wooded to the water's edge. Along the
west shore a dry swamp of spruce and tamarack extended,
and a semicircular range of hills, bounding a small prairie
below us, came around to where we lay."

In the distance, looking to the north and the narrows, Steele could see people wading through the water, struggling eastward and clearly in a hurry. Gazing through his binoculars, Steele also noticed several Natives ambling about the half-dozen teepees set up in this "small prairie." One woman patiently tended a teapot suspended over a small fire. Numerous wagons and carts were scattered about the camp, some lying in a broken, derelict state.

Steele and Butlin quietly slipped back from their vantage point and returned to the men. The dismounted Scouts gathered around their leader, who jumped up on a large rock to outline his plan of action. Steele advised his men he intended to advance on the teepees on foot, allowing Reverend McKay a chance to demand in Cree that the Natives surrender. If all went well, the Natives would release the remaining prisoners alive. If they refused to surrender and shooting started, Steele prepared his force to split into two groups. The group under Steele's command would charge the teepees, searching for the prisoners, while the second group, under the command of Sergeant William Fury, would be responsible for protecting Steele's group from any rifle fire coming from the surrounding ridge. Should the prisoners not be found immediately, Steele planned to force the Cree out of the village and across the narrows so the Scouts could identify and separate the prisoners. Steele had the men "number off," with the even numbers being in his group and the odd numbers going with Fury. Two very disappointed injured Scouts—Jumbo Fisk likely being one of them—would be left to guard the tied-up horses. Joseph Hicks, a member of the Scouts, recorded in his journal that there were only 47 men making the attack, going up against what they erroneously believed to be over 200 Cree warriors, an estimate arrived at by counting over 50 campfires at the last Cree camp.

The Scouts checked their Winchesters and ammunition in preparation for the coming encounter. In a single group, with Steele in the lead, the force advanced down the slope toward the camp; it was now 10:00 AM. At first, they advanced cautiously, trying not to appear that they were charging into the camp and hoping to give McKay his opportunity to call out to the teepees. Unfortunately, the Scouts stumbled upon several Cree guards concealed in the trees near the bottom of the hill, and these warriors immediately opened fire on them. The sound of shooting raised the alarm for every Cree within hearing distance, so Steele immediately shouted an order to form into the two planned assault groups. Steele and 23 men from the first group charged toward the village, holding their fire for fear of shooting one of the prisoners. They raced through the teepees, ripping open the doors, quickly glancing into the interiors and taking several surprised Natives, both male and female, as prisoners, and apparently wounding at least one man in the process. Once the teepees were cleared, they turned to the enemy, who began materializing out of the

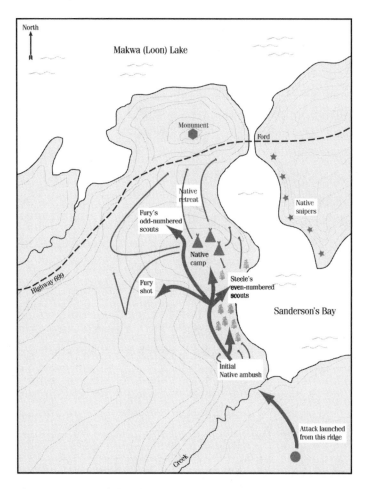

The positions of Steele's Scouts and the Cree during the skirmish at Loon Lake. TOM HOWELL

trees along the lakeshore. The confrontation quickly became a "fastest man on the trigger" firefight.

Meanwhile, William Fury's team moved past the teepees and spread out, assaulting the hillside. Warriors took up positions to fire down on them from the ridgetop, and Fury knew, outnumbered as the Scouts were, they had to clear it immediately. In addition, the warriors were manoeuvring closer to where the Scouts' horses were tied. If the Scouts were cut off from their horses and surrounded, they would find themselves in a defensive position from which there'd be no escape. Fury shouted orders and encouragement to his men as they struggled up the slope, slipping and sliding back as they went, their leather-soled cowboy boots failing to provide traction on the grass. As Fury neared the top, along with Reverend McKay, John Corryell and Albert McDonell, a bullet smashed through his chest, searing him with pain and knocking him to the ground.

Weekwaypan, the Metis sharpshooting buffalo hunter who had been so dangerous to the field-gun team at Frenchman Butte, was again causing havoc. A .50-calibre bullet fired by Weekwaypan had penetrated the right side of Fury's chest, the heavy slug going right through his body. McKay was at Fury's side in an instant, rolling him over and opening up his jacket. McKay whipped off his handkerchief, rolled it into a dressing and pressed it onto the wound to stem the bleeding. As McKay bandaged Fury, he gave the wounded man a few encouraging words, assuring him he wasn't going to die. Promising to return in a few minutes, McKay picked up his rifle and scrambled off uphill.

The Scouts succeeded in forcing the Cree to retreat along the ridge, back northward toward the narrows as planned. Having cleared the teepees and discovering that none of the prisoners were in the camp, Steele's group was now coming under fire from warriors situated along the shoreline willows close to the lake. The Scouts responded by wheeling about to sweep them back north toward the narrows. The fighting was intense, and with no clear battle lines it was every man for himself. A warrior jumped out from hiding less than three metres in front of Scout William Fielders, who instinctively fired in a split second, killing the man. In another incident, a Scout who was standing behind a tree unknowingly exposed his shoulders and arms on each side, and a bullet smacked harmlessly into the tree trunk, dead centre. The rapid firing made the barrels of the Scouts' Winchesters so hot that they became difficult to grip without gloves. Steele later wrote his version of how the battle progressed:

> They [Cree warriors] posted themselves under the shelter of the hills opposite to us and again opened fire, their bullets tearing the bark off the trees 'round my trumpeter, Chabot, and myself. Chabot offered me his rifle to fire at the red men, who seemed to be making fine practice, but I told him to go ahead as I had something else to do and a few minutes later I heard an Indian Chief [Wandering Spirit] leading his men

with yells of encouragement around the hills to my left front, and to meet the attack sent by the men [Fury's group] on my left up the hill.

As soon as the battle commenced, the rifle fire was heard all the way to the main Cree camp, located out of sight across the narrows and over a kilometre away to the east. The warriors in the camp grabbed their rifles, many having nothing more than old smooth-bore muzzleloaders, and rushed toward the fighting. Unable to cross the water, they began sniping at the Scouts from the opposite side of the narrows, a distance of about 300 metres. Without protection on the far shore, they were vulnerable to the Scouts' modern Winchesters; consequently, two were killed and others wounded.

In a separate incident at the main camp, the highly respected chief of the Onion Lake Band, Seekaskootch ("Cut Arm"), an amputee, rushed about trying to persuade his people to surrender. Seekaskootch was a bearded Metis living as a Native. He threatened, "I will shoot anyone who fires at a white man!" then turned and dashed into his teepee to get his headdress and weapon. Upon emerging from his teepee, he was shot in the back of the head by Little Poplar, a militant Plains Cree warrior and a nephew of Big Bear. Years later, Seekaskootch's son, Missehew, spoke of those moments, "I ran across a dead Indian [his father] and when we checked he had been shot with a small bore rifle, we went on and found another wounded man. He told us it wasn't soldiers that got them." It's possible that old grudges manifested themselves in convenient revenge killings during the conflict, and some deaths may not have been directly related to the battle.

Missehew continued, "They [Steele's Scouts] are good shots. My brother took his leggings and put them on a stick, lifting them up. Immediately there were three shots, and three bullet holes appeared in the leggings. One of the three doing the shooting was a left hander with a crooked nose. After he shot, he would get up and turn around slowly before disappearing. My brother took careful aim at this man and shot at him."

At about this point in the battle, Scout William West was shot in the leg, the bullet entering his kneecap and lodging in his thigh. Although the wound was debilitating, West was later able to mount his horse and ride until he reached the ambulances and medical staff of General Middleton's column.

Back at the narrows, Kitty McLean braved a fusillade of bullets as she waded across the ford with water over her waist, passing the floating body of a Cree warrior, Osawan, shot only moments before. She carried her 18-month-old brother, John, in her arms. A bullet zipped past, going between her head and John's, causing her to involuntarily jerk back. The shawl draped over her head fell back and revealed her identity to the Scouts, who, at that point in the conflict, were firing at anything that moved. A shout went up, "Cease fire, cease fire! My God, those are the prisoners!" The shooting stopped momentarily, and when it resumed the Scouts were more careful when they fired upon anyone wading in the water.

For the Cree, the situation was desperate. Many of the warriors had little or no ammunition left. Some of those using the old muzzleloading smooth-bore muskets were reduced to picking up stones from the lakeshore to use in place of lead balls. Several of the Cree warriors, pressured into retreating from the ridge to the narrows, came to an open, grassy meadow that exposed them to the sharpshooting Scouts now positioned on the ridge to the south. There was nothing they could do but dash across this "little prairie" in an attempt to escape to the water. Each in turn made the sprint, and each was struck by Scout rifle fire. Three Cree warriors were killed: Komenakos, Mestahekpinpiko and Pawacemocees. In addition, several unidentified Natives were wounded but survived their desperate rush across the opening.

The battle came to a stalemate, just as it had at Frenchman Butte, the Cree on one side of the hill with their backs toward the narrows crossing, and the Scouts on the other side facing them. The two forces were close enough they could shout insults back and forth, fearing to stick their heads up to fire at the enemy. Scout Joseph Hicks recalled hearing the moaning of wounded warriors on the opposite side, and some of the Scouts began hollering at the Cree over the crest, accusing them of killing helpless women and children. The reply, Hicks claimed, was that the Scouts could go to "Indian Hell!"

Steele asked Reverend McKay to call out for the Cree to surrender, which he attempted three times, only to be met by flying bullets on each occasion. Meanwhile, on the other side, similar attempts at calling for a truce were made by William McLean, also at great risk and without success; unrecognized by the Scouts, he too faced bullets. Cree warriors, fearing they'd be held responsible for his death, finally pulled him down for his own safety.

With the battle in abeyance, Steele canvassed his men on the status of their ammunition. Some of them were down to only a handful of cartridges, and it soon became obvious to him that a successful rescue of the prisoners was unlikely. In addition, unaware of the enemy's severe lack of ammunition and lacking the reinforcements and ammunition promised earlier by General Strange, Steele concluded the safety of his men would be jeopardized by remaining on the scene. He had little choice but to withdraw.

Steele ordered his men to begin pulling back to the horses. As they passed through the camp, they set fire to the Cree teepees, confiscated a buckboard to carry several wounded men and picked up a few axes for use on the trail as they returned southward. The column remounted their horses, and Steele stood by in his tattered red tunic and white hat doing a head count as they passed by him. Steele ordered six men and an officer to remain behind on the hill as rearguard protection. He took a last look at the scene below and reluctantly turned his horse's head to follow the column, knowing they'd failed—again.

The rearguard remained at the rock as ordered, built a fire and fired off an occasional shot to remind the Cree that the Scouts were still present. The men busied themselves heating up water for tea as tinned bully-beef rations warmed in the coals. They dipped hardtack biscuits into the tea and munched them along with the bully beef, their first food of the day. They lingered around the fire through the rest of the day, then slipped away in the deepening twilight of evening.

Official records say that five Natives were killed in the Loon Lake skirmish, but in his report to General Strange at the end of the campaign, Steele indicates his group killed five while Fury's contingent killed seven. It is unknown how many wounded Natives later died from their wounds.

The Scouts followed the same trail they had travelled on their way to Loon Lake. About 10 kilometres along the route, they met the point scouts from General Middleton's force in the early evening. Middleton had been methodically progressing along in a dogged effort to catch up to Steele's force, dragging the Gatling guns with him. In the proper military fashion, Steele lined up his mounted men beside the trail and saluted his superior as the pompous general rode past.

The Loon Lake Melee

Lewis Redman Ord, a rifleman with the Queen's Own Rifles survey scouts, later wrote of the impression Steele's Scouts made as they presented themselves for Middleton:

A few miles on we found Steele and his command—that officer not having been able to follow up his advantage from lack of supplies and ammunition and at once notice[d] the genius and forethought required to make a force march with due regard for proprieties. What a vast advantage education confers on a man; here is Steele, a poor ignorant devil of a Canadian, with his seventy men away up in this blasted, howling wilderness, you know, and no wagons, no tents, no comforts; positively nothing, you know. We come upon a little open patch and see drawn up and waiting for us Major Steele's troop of mounted men, bronzed by sun and wind and toughened by hardship and exposure. Led by a MAN and unencumbered by red tape, they pushed rapidly after these Indians, fought and beaten them and, after waiting vainly for support for two days, were now ready to show us the way. Truly they are like the scouts one used to read about, yet beyond some lines barely mentioned the fight; I have seen nothing written of this plucky officer and his command.

Middleton decided the force should camp early to rest and feed the horses, then continue on the next morning. The wounded Scouts—Fielders, Fisk and Fury—were immediately taken back to Fort Pitt in an ambulance wagon, along with the shackled Cree prisoners captured by the Scouts during the attack. In his journal entries,

Middleton complains of the horrific conditions he was forced to endure, including dastardly bulldogs, mosquitos and swampy terrain, which he found appalling. He begrudgingly concluded they must struggle on beyond the scene of the skirmish and doggedly pursue the Cree to the very end. Highly displeased at Steele for launching his "flying pursuit" of the running Cree, he positioned the Scouts at the very rear of his column as a rebuke to Steele for failing to wait for his "supreme commander." It didn't seem to matter to Middleton that Steele had embarked on the foray under General Strange's orders. In the morning, they forded the narrows, leaving their two Gatling guns and gun crews behind in the camp.

After continuing northward partway around the lake-shore, two of the Scouts came across the body of a Native woman, Sits by the Door, hanging from the limb of a tree. Kitty McLean (later Mrs. K.M. Yuille) described the woman's demise in notes for a speech she delivered to Northwest Rebellion veterans in Toronto in April 1935:

> Just before we started for the swamp [just beyond the second narrows on the north end of Loon Lake], I noticed a woman who was a cripple, her knees being bent so that she could neither stand or walk. She was sitting under a big tree, with her little dog in her lap, where she had evidently crawled after being [carried across] a stream. She was such a refined, placid looking woman, who always made me think of a nice lady. She dressed so nicely and had such a well groomed

appearance. Her hair was always done smoothly and she always had some bright remark to make to those who passed by. She had had a cart to ride in until it had to be given up as there was no road; then she rode in a travois until that had to be abandoned on account of the density of the bush; then she was helped on her pony and rode horse-back, but now some-one had stolen her pony. Here we found her three weeks later on our return [after being finally freed by the Cree]. She had hanged herself by reaching up to a big limb just over her head, and had used her belt to hang herself by! And so we found her with her little dog dead by her side. THREE WEEKS! It was not a pretty sight.

The trail led east along the lakeshore then bent northward in a semi-circle to a second narrows on the north side of the lake. Here Middleton's survey scouts (engineers) commenced to build a bridge, which was never completed, while the mounted Steele's Scouts obediently accompanied Middleton's cavalry and forded the narrows, only to find the terrain almost impassible on horseback. Middleton's horse wandered slightly off the trail and floundered in the muck, nearly going down and dumping the general as it stumbled and thrashed about. This crowning indignity convinced Middleton to abandon the pursuit. The force turned around and made their way back west to the narrows battle site, then on toward Fort Pitt. They had failed once again to free the prisoners.

CHAPTER

Searching for Will-o'-the-Wisps

THE FLEEING CREE HAD SPLIT into two groups, the Woods Cree travelling north in a gigantic arc from Loon Lake, turning west along the shore of Lac des Isles. Just south of today's town of Goodsoil, the remaining prisoners were set free. Provided with a limited supply of food, a gun and an ox, they were instructed to find their way back down the trail just travelled, back to Fort Pitt.

Near starvation, the remaining Cree sustained themselves by shooting rabbits and catching spawning fish in the creeks leading to the lakes while making their way toward the Cold Lake area in the hopes of acquiring food from the trading post at Beaver Crossing. The second group, including most of the militant Plains Cree, turned south and travelled across the prairie to Montana, never to return. At about this time, Big Bear left the group, accompanied by his youngest son, Horse-child. The two travelled southeast toward Fort Carlton, intent on surrendering to the white soldiers.

Middleton hoped to confront the Cree by coming at them from the west, so he ordered General Strange to march with all haste to the post on the Beaver River and establish a base with access to the Beaver and Cold Rivers, as well as the Pierce Lake and Lac des Isles drainage chain. Utilizing these waterways, he planned to hunt down the remaining Cree and conclude the campaign in one final battle.

On June 3, Strange and his diminished Alberta Field Force, lacking Steele and the Scouts, who were now attached to Middleton's force at Loon Lake, marched to Frog Lake and camped near the creek at the south end of the lake. Resuming the march the next morning, they soon discovered the trail deteriorated into a sodden quagmire. The force pushed across the morass of seemingly endless swamps and muskegs, passing Rita and Angling Lakes on the way. The 65th Mount Royal Rifles, wearing worn-out boots made of poor quality leather, suffered the worst, and many of the soldiers resorted to walking barefoot through the mosquito-infested swamps. To add to their misery, the nine-pound field gun used in the Battle of Frenchman Butte accompanied them as an additional burden. To their credit, they hauled the heavy field piece and its caisson and never flagged from the marching pace of the force. In one instance, they disassembled the gun and slid the naked barrel backwards on the end of several ropes to cross a huge muskeg, then reassembled it on the far side of the ooze. For their determination and vigour, the other soldiers dubbed them "the Alligators," a great source of pride to the encumbered men.

After marching through the night, Strange's force reached the Beaver River post, on the south bank of the river. As they arrived, Strange spotted a group of Chipewyan braves, who had split from the Cree at Frenchman Butte, also making for the store. The Alberta Field Force had beaten them to their goal by only a few short minutes. General Strange secured the site and delegated a small contingent of Winnipeg Light Infantry to remain there as a guard. The rest of the force continued east for another 10 kilometres to the Roman Catholic mission at Le Goff. When he arrived, Strange found the small community abandoned and completely ransacked in the absence of its resident priest, Father Le Goff. Strange established his militia base camp here, commandeering several homes, one of which became his headquarters while others were disrespectfully converted into latrines for the soldiers.

On June 7, Father Le Goff appeared out of the wilderness with a small group of his faithful, and Strange was able to solicit his aid in searching out other Chipewyan families hiding in the countryside. Strange stipulated they must come in peaceably and surrender over the next few days; most of them complied with the demand. The surrender revealed the pathetic situation of the Chipewyan. As Strange watched them surrender their guns, he saw that nearly all of them were worn-out muzzleloading muskets, with only a few repaired Winchesters that had been left behind by Dickens at Fort Pitt. Despite the guns' damaged condition, somehow the ingenious warriors had succeeded in repairing a few of them.

General Strange established a court of inquiry to evaluate Chipewyan involvement in the uprising. During the inquiry, he learned that most of the men had little involvement in the events at Fort Pitt and Frenchman Butte. To his astonishment, several testified that the Plains Cree warriors had convinced them that at the conclusion of the uprising, a large portion of western Canada would be sold by the Metis to the United States. They were told that only those who joined the uprising would receive any money from the sale, so they fell in with the rebels.

After abandoning his pursuit of Big Bear at Loon Lake, General Middleton redirected his force. Bypassing their Fort Pitt base, he marched directly west to Frog Lake following an old, rarely used trail that passed north of Onion Lake. Picking up Strange's track, he turned north following it to Le Goff. While Strange awaited Middleton's arrival, his troops began constructing several small scow-like boats, intending to descend the Beaver River to intercept the fractured Cree force camped somewhere in the Lac des Isles area. This operation was later cancelled when Strange confirmed from scouting reports and the inquiry testimony that the enemy had fragmented into small groups and fled in several directions.

Strange, acting in accordance with General Middleton's plan of attack, sent Colonel Osborne-Smith, commanding 100 men of the Winnipeg Light Infantry, to Cold Lake. From there, Smith intended to commandeer Chipewyan canoes and paddle eastward in parallel with the Beaver River scows. He planned to follow the south shore of Cold Lake, enter the Cold River and continue downstream into Pierce Lake and Lac des Isles. Once Steele and his Scouts detected the enemy, the two forces would attack the remaining Cree in a pincer movement.

The Winnipeg Light Infantry hacked its way north through dense bush, following along the west side of Cold Lake's Long Bay until they reached the lakeshore. They established their camp on a narrow beach directly across from today's Cold Lake Provincial Park boat launch. Upon reaching the shore, the unit was under orders to remain there until General Middleton caught up with them. This gave the weary soldiers a day or two off, and they spent their time washing, swimming and taking exploratory shoreline walks around the point to Garnet Beach. Some of the men rigged up lines and a net to do a little fishing from shore and off crude rafts. The catch of fresh fish augmented their tiresome rations.

On June 7, Captain R.W. Rutherford of the Canadian Artillery painted a watercolour depicting General Middleton engaged in a shoreline conversation at Cold Lake with General Strange, while Osborne-Smith lingers in the background. This painting was one of a number created by Rutherford that portray scenes from the campaign. After this discussion, General Middleton concluded there was no point in continuing the pursuit because all the available information indicated the Cree had dispersed widely and would be impossible to intercept. The next morning, he ordered his force to withdraw from their most northerly advance in the campaign and march back to Le Goff.

The force remained at the camp for the rest of the day, and General Middleton commandeered a Native's canoe to do some angling himself. One soldier indicates he fished in Long Bay and "caught a few," thus becoming the first "celebrity tourist" to visit the future resort of Cold Lake. Steele and his Scouts, under the thumb of General Middleton, were clearly still out of favour and held on a short leash. Relegated to obeying orders to the letter, the Scouts were limited to inconsequential patrols downstream along the Beaver River, all of which proved fruitless.

At about this time, a messenger arrived at Fort Pitt with the news that the Cree, encumbered by the responsibility of the white prisoners, had finally set them free on June 18, just south of Goodsoil. It would take over two days for the released prisoners to make their way back to the narrows battle site before being discovered by roaming scouts. They eventually reached Fort Pitt around dawn on June 24, safe at last. The prisoners' release brought an end to the militia's campaign. The western prairies could now be turned over for settlement. The Wild West was forever dead, and the great adventure was over.

On June 25 at Le Goff, reveille sounded just before dawn. After breakfast, the entire force assembled into their ranks to march back to Fort Pitt. The Scouts had one last chance to escape Middleton's scrutiny. An unconfirmed report of disturbing incidents occurring at Frog Lake obliged Middleton to respond, so he reluctantly ordered the Scouts to ride ahead of the marching column to investigate. Once again, however, the information proved false, but the report freed the Scouts to continue back to Fort Pitt by themselves, enjoying their own company.

The Scouts languished at Fort Pitt for weeks, absorbed into a swelling militia camp that numbered over 2,100 soldiers. The Scouts looked despicable, more like a group of ragtag, long-haired beggars than a militia, their clothing dirty, shredded and torn beyond repair. The meals served at the camp were almost inedible, often consisting of rancid pork that was so bad that most of the men wouldn't have offered it to their dog back home. A few of the more destitute Scouts resorted to cutting arm and neck holes in flour sacks to make shirts. Their boots were so worn they had to lash the tops onto the soles with flour-sack twine. Steele did everything he could, short of thievery, to improve conditions but grew more disillusioned over their predicament with each passing day. The horses were also in terrible condition. After existing on prairie and swamp grass for two months, they looked like they were starving, some showing their ribs like rafters on a new house. Gradually, given regular good feed, the Scouts' mounts recovered.

Many Scouts took up the pastime of angling in the river, even though fishermen were lined up along the bank shoulder to shoulder. Horse racing also proved popular among the entire military force. Betting ran high at these races and IOUs and personal items changed hands because of the lack of cash.

With each dawn and reveille, the troops wondered if it would be the day they went home. Finally, on June 29, the first contingent marched aboard the sternwheeler *Marquis*, and with a farewell blast of its whistle it turned about in the current and headed downstream.

The 65th Mount Royal Rifles held a joyous reunion on July 3 when their battalion brothers from Forts Normandeau, Ostell and Ethier marched into camp. They had spent the previous months diligently guarding the major river crossings on the supply route between Calgary and Edmonton. With their duties fulfilled, they closed the forts down and marched cross-country to Fort Pitt.

Nearly all the Alberta Field Force troops departed from Fort Pitt on July 4 aboard the sternwheelers *North West* and

NWMP members of Steele's Scouts, photographed in August 1885 at Fort Battleford. Back row, from left to right: Kerr, Walters, Fane, Waring, A. Davidson, Morton, Hetherington, Whipps, Percival. Centre row, from left to right: Sergeant Fury, Robinson, Dubreuil, Bunt. Front row, reclining, from left to right: Richardson, McMinn, Sergeant McRae, McCarthy. Fane and McCarthy were not officially signed on as Scouts. GLENBOW ARCHIVES NA-936-22

Baroness. As the boats ran downstream, they dodged sandbars and shallow water, arriving at Fort Battleford the next day. As they departed from Fort Pitt, a July snow squall blew in, causing havoc with the boats as they cast off and tried to turn in the wind and current. One normally pious soldier groused in his letter home, "It is impossible to avoid swearing in this part of Canada, the nature of the climate enforces the desire. One day in July the temperature is in the 90's [°F] the next a snow storm."

The NWMP members of the Scouts from Calgary also

boarded the riverboats for Fort Battleford, so it was the Scouts' final morning together as a group. After a layover of a few days in Fort Battleford, the NWMP Scouts travelled by steamboat along the North Saskatchewan to its most southerly point, 20 kilometres from Saskatoon, where it bends in a 90-degree angle to flow northeast until, about 35 kilometres past Prince Albert, it reaches its confluence with the South Saskatchewan River. At this point, vessels turned upstream on the South Saskatchewan to steam on to Swift Current. Here, passengers transferred onto trains that either travelled east or headed west to Calgary.

Steele led the column of remaining Scouts from Edmonton and Calgary as they returned on horseback to their homes. When they reached Edmonton, the four Steele brothers, Sam, Godfrey, Richard and James were together for a few short hours; there is no record of such a family reunion ever happening again.

CHAPTER

9

The End of an Era

ON THE MORNING OF JULY 18, Calgary's mayor, George Murdock, was out for a morning ride north of the rapidly growing town of Calgary when he spotted the Scouts' column eagerly trotting south on the trail from Edmonton. He didn't wait to meet them as he knew full well who they were. He spun his horse around and galloped for town. Thundering at full speed down Stephen Avenue, he shouted out to the gawking bystanders, "The boys are coming, the boys are coming—they'll be here within the hour!"

Pandemonium erupted as people rushed to spread the word and get ready for the arrival of the Scouts. In anticipation of their return, the community had several days earlier erected a huge arch over Stephen Avenue. It featured a massive welcome banner strung across the top, and a speakers' podium stood beneath it. As Steele's Scouts forded the Bow River, it was almost time for the welcome party.

It must have been a proud moment for Sam Steele as he led his battle-veteran Scouts under the arch. He glanced about and guessed nearly every person in Calgary was there, waving and showing smiles a mile wide. Cheers went up, and the clapping seemed unending. Steele dismounted and joined a beckoning Mayor Murdock on the platform; the two shook hands to more cheers. Between rounds of cheering, Murdock, an excellent orator, sincerely welcomed the Scouts and praised them for "coming out of the fight with credit and honour."

Steele gave a short, modest response, thanking the mayor for recognizing his men and stating that each and every one of them was proud to have served in a time of turmoil. To conclude the initial ceremony, three cheers were given for the Scouts and then another round went up for the queen before the crowd began to disperse.

Several days later, the community hosted a gigantic banquet honouring the Scouts, even though the NWMP Scout members were still on their way by river and rail. An estimated 350 guests jammed into the Boynton Hall to join the celebration. Numerous speeches and presentations were made by local dignitaries. Mayor Murdock presented Sam with a diamond ring, given on behalf of the appreciative citizens of Calgary in recognition of his leadership and service. Steele rose and replied eloquently, emphasizing that, unlike the other Scouts, he had not volunteered, but had been ordered to serve as the Scouts' commander. He instead acknowledged the service of the volunteer members who had so diligently pursued the rebels. To say the evening was a boisterous celebration would be a gross understatement. A number of overexuberant attendees, as that week's issue of the newspaper put it, spent the latter part of the evening in the local jail, "sleeping it off."

Every Scout was paid $2.50 for each day of his service by Steele himself, then they went on their way, most to be lost to history. Some months later, they would all receive their service medal for the campaign—a round disk inscribed with "Northwest 1885" and "Canada." The medal was suspended on a ribbon and clasp. Recipients who came under fire had an additional clasp inscribed "Saskatchewan" clipped to the ribbon, just above the medal.

On the day he was awarded his service medal, Steele received a telegram directly from the NWMP controller in Ottawa, Fred White, promoting him to the rank of superintendent. This promotion had been a long time coming for Steele, since advancement in the force during this period of NWMP history was usually awarded for political achievements. In Steele's case, it was grudgingly awarded for his professional attributes and exceptional service.

In 1888, Steele led a contingent of police to the Kootenays of British Columbia, settling Native unrest there and building the fort named after him. He married Marie Lotbinière-Harwood in 1890, and they raised a family of three children. In 1898, Steele was posted to Yukon, taking command of all law enforcement in the territory during the Klondike Gold Rush. It would be Steele's last NWMP posting. In 1899, Steele resigned from his beloved force and became the first commanding officer of Lord Strathcona's Horse (now a tank regiment based in Edmonton). This cavalry regiment included many ex-Scouts, who accompanied him overseas to serve during the Boer War in South Africa. After the end of the Boer War, Steele remained behind to assist in developing the South African Constabulary, which he patterned after the NWMP. With the outbreak of the First World War, Steele accepted a position in the Canadian army as a major general of the Canadian 2nd Division, based in England. He was not allowed to visit the trenches on the continent for fear he'd be killed. Steele served in England until the war ended in 1918. Shortly after, he finally received the recognition he deserved when he marched before King George V and was awarded a knighthood. This icon of Canadian law enforcement would now be addressed as Sir Samuel Benfield Steele. Steele passed away after contracting influenza during an epidemic in January of 1919; he was buried in Winnipeg with the full military honours due to a truly great Canadian hero.

General Thomas Bland "Jingo" Strange accompanied Alberta Field Force members on the riverboats to Swift

Current, where the militia boarded an overcrowded train going east, and Strange and the NWMP headed west. Strange and many of the others became embroiled in a pay-and-benefits conflict with Ottawa at the conclusion of hostilities. Ottawa claimed that Strange had forfeited his military pension when he accepted the position of general in the Alberta Field Force. It was several years before he was finally awarded his pension. Strange's huge cattle ranch near Gleichen ultimately failed from neglect after Strange suffered a permanently debilitating broken leg that never healed properly. Eventually, Jingo became the premier sales representative for Maxim machine guns, touring much of the world selling this revolutionary weapon to a variety of governments during the First World War. He died in England in 1925. Strange's autobiography, *Gunner Jingo's Jubilee*, includes a useful, detailed account of his experiences during the Northwest Rebellion.

The fighting preacher, George McKay, returned to Calgary with the rest of the Scouts before continuing home to Fort Macleod. McKay also ran into a bureaucratic battle over his benefits with Ottawa. The government insisted he served as a member of the clergy and therefore did not qualify for any benefits or pay other than the service medal. A few years later, at Sam Steele's urging, he accepted the position of Indian Agent west of Calgary, where he gained high respect from the Native people. He eventually moved to South Dakota, where he attained the title of archdeacon.

He died peacefully, unlike some other frontiersmen, at age 85 in 1949. McKay wrote an autobiography, *The Fighting Preacher*, but only rare typed copies exist, most buried deep in government archives.

The aptly named William Fury was a very competent frontier Mountie who survived being shot in the chest during the fighting at Loon Lake. He was left with a collapsed lung, which limited his ability to exert himself, so he applied for invalid status and left the NWMP in 1888. His pension application was strongly supported by a recommendation from his commanding officer, Sam Steele, and the medical officers of the Force. He was awarded an uncontested pension and took up farming near Richmond Hill, Ontario, where he died in 1936. He was buried with full military honours in Killean, Ontario.

William Parker served as a Mountie for 38 years before retiring to become a real-estate agent in Medicine Hat. In his later years, he became a colourful storyteller about town, often referred to as "Bullshit Parker." He died in 1945 at age 92 and is buried in Medicine Hat.

Joseph Butlin, the man who is believed to have shot Meminook, was one of the original NWMP enlistees in 1873, riding with Steele in the Great March West but soon leaving the force for better opportunities. In 1885, he owned a stone quarry near Calgary, which he operated until 1901. He later moved to Wetaskiwin to become an employee of Pat Burns, a wealthy rancher and member of the Calgary

Stampede's famous Big Four, and eventually accepted an Indian Agent position at Hobbema. Joe and his wife raised 10 children. He died in 1930.

Like the proverbial old soldier, most of the other Scouts, including Sam's brothers Richard and Godfrey, have just faded away into the past. But at least one outspoken Scout told of his memories of the rebellion. Ralph Bell was about 24 years old in 1885. He was still a lively old-timer in 1953, residing in Calgary. He died shortly after an article he wrote appeared in the December 1953 issue of *Saskatchewan Farmer*. In the article, he describes the rebellion as "that racket" and refers to Sam Steele by his nickname of "Ol' Smoothbore." The eccentric Bell certainly had little love for General Middleton; he insisted, "There wasn't a bigger jackass in the country than him, and the whole thing could have been averted."

In addition to the members of Steele's Scouts, others who played a role in the 1885 rebellion deserve attention. Chief Trader William McLean continued to work for the HBC until he retired around 1892. He continued to lead an active life and conducted a secretive study of "alcohol and criminal activity amongst indigenous peoples," for the Department of Indian Affairs. Like many others, he sought out his fortune and failed in the Yukon Gold Rush in 1899. Little is known about his life after this time other than he was still connected with the Department of Indian Affairs when he died in 1929.

The End of an Era

Amelia McLean, Canada's Annie Oakley, attended university and after graduating spent many years connected with the Department of Indian Affairs, where she used her exceptional Aboriginal linguistic skills. In 1899, she married Frederick Paget and moved to Ottawa. She continued her relationship with Indian Affairs by travelling throughout the West. She is said to have travelled entirely on her own, camping out in a tent while interviewing Native elders and recording stories that became the basis for her book *The People of the Plains*, published in 1909. She passed away in the summer of 1922 at her father's home in Winnipeg. Katherine "Kitty" McLean married to become Mrs. K.M. Yuille. In April 1935, she gave a speech to Northwest Rebellion veterans at their 50-year reunion in Toronto. Of the other eight McLean children, including Elizabeth, little is known. The McLeans were a unique and very capable frontier family; if their story were ever fully researched and told, it would undoubtedly provide exciting reading.

Of the First Nations warriors who participated in the rebellion, seven were convicted of murder. One, Louison Mongrain, won a reprieve for his diligence in protecting the captive women during their time in the Cree camp. The six others responsible for the Frog Lake murders—Round-the-Sky, Bad Arrow, Miserable Man, Iron Body, Little Bear and Wandering Spirit—were sentenced to the disgraceful death they dreaded. They were publicly hanged at Fort Battleford on November 27, 1885. Their bodies were unceremoniously loaded into a wagon and transported to a mass grave. This grave is situated over the crest of the valley, below today's public campground, northeast of the fort. There is a monument at the gravesite, and visitors will discover that these individuals have not been forgotten by their community. There are always small commemorative offerings left on the monument that honours them.

On July 2, 1885, an exhausted, aged and exceedingly filthy Mistahimaskwa—Big Bear—accompanied by his young son, Horse-child, surrendered to a surprised NWMP sergeant, William Smart, who had been detailed to the boring routine of guarding a river ferry not far from Fort Carlton. General Strange sagely commented that Smart was about the only man not searching for the notorious Big Bear. The prisoner was taken to Prince Albert where he was compelled to take a bath and undergo a demeaning lice-preventing haircut while he awaited his trial on charges of treason. In prison, he became a bewildered showpiece on display. Nearly every man in the settlement clamoured to see him whenever he was on his daily exercise walk inside the prison. He also silently endured the additional humiliation of wearing handcuffs and leg shackles whenever he wasn't locked in his damp, cold cell. Big Bear suffered from a deep depression, and his health deteriorated quickly. He was released because of his poor health, serving only a portion of his three-year sentence. He went back to the Little Pine Reserve, west of Battleford, where he lived until his death in 1888.

Like Big Bear, most Native leaders recognized the treaties to be a bad deal. As difficult as the situation was in the years leading up to the rebellion, it became much worse after 1885. The Canadian government's goal seems to have been to forever put such fear into "the Indian" that they would never, ever, consider standing up for themselves against the government in the future. All guns, ammunition, horses, carts, wagons and harnesses were taken from them at the conclusion of the rebellion. All males, including chiefs and councillors, were required to register; they were virtually under house arrest and confined to the boundaries of their reserves. They were required to carry a written permit each time they left their reserves for any reason, and in some locations this restriction existed well into the 1960s. In addition, Native children were arbitrarily taken from their homes and placed in residential schools that separated them from their families and culture. In recent years, First Nations people have regained some control over their lives, but there is still a long way to go in their journey toward equality in Canada.

Appendix:
Following the Trail of 1885

The Northwest Rebellion, often today called the Northwest Resistance, is a hugely intriguing period in western Canadian history. There are many points of interest associated with the events of 1885 that may be visited and explored today. Those who would like to follow the trail of Steele's Scouts in 1885 should begin their journey at www.trailsof1885.ca. This website is a gateway to information about the historical sites of the Northwest Rebellion.

The story of Steele's Scouts begins at Fort Calgary Historic Site, at the confluence of the Bow and Elbow Rivers. The site features an interpretive centre, the NWMP barracks and reconstructed portions of the original fort. Unfortunately, none of the Alberta Field Force's overnight camps travelling north on the 1885 Edmonton Trail are identified, despite being located close to the old Highway 2, which meanders through several towns as it makes its way north to Edmonton. Just west of Red Deer is a reconstruction of Fort Normandeau, where, during the summer months, the staff sometimes dress in period militia costume. To the north, neither Fort Ostell nor Fort Ethier are identified, even though the original 1885 blockhouse at Fort Ethier still exists.

At Edmonton, the modern Alberta Legislative Buildings stand on the grounds of old Fort Edmonton, so a new fort and heritage centre have been developed beside the North Saskatchewan River on the west side of the city. This popular complex portrays several time periods in Edmonton's colourful past, including 1885 Street, which reflects the rebellion period.

The Alberta Field Force followed the Carlton/Edmonton Trail, a Red River cart "highway" throughout the 1800s that roughly paralleled the North Saskatchewan River. Victoria Settlement, the site of the climax of the white horse legend, is an Alberta provincial historic site located south of the town of Smoky Lake on the banks of the North Saskatchewan. From here, the trail led east through Saddle Lake First Nations Reserve and right through the town of St. Paul to Elk Point. About eight kilometres east of Elk Point is the Fort George and Buckingham House Provincial Historic Site and interpretive centre. Although no longer in existence in 1885, these important twin forts were visited by many famous explorers during the fur-trade era.

Frog Lake Settlement, scene of the multiple murders that triggered the western portion of the Northwest Rebellion, is located approximately 40 kilometres east of the town of Elk Point, near the Fishing Lake Metis Colony. This historic site consists of a tidy, fenced compound with a monument and grave markers. Across the gravel road to the south is a walking trail with interpretive signs that introduce visitors to the tragic events that occurred there in 1885. It takes diligent exploring, using good historic references as a guide, to discover the original basements of the 1885 buildings, all of which are purposely left unmarked and lie concealed in the dense underbrush.

Fort Pitt, the closest fort to Frog Lake, is now a Saskatchewan provincial park. At the site, timbers are pinned to the ground identifying the outlines of the original fort and the one that replaced it. There are also interpretive signs and a pleasant day-use area beside the river. A palisade-like compound marks the perimeter of the original graveyard of both of the forts. The graves are unmarked since the tombstones were removed during the 1885 conflict. This compound was constructed and named "God's Half Acre" by a local homesteading rancher, Robert Hougham, as a tribute to its occupants.

Down the road about 15 kilometres to the east is the hamlet of Frenchman Butte and its renowned heritage centre and museum (www.frenchmanbuttemuseum.ca), which features a collection of about eight heritage buildings, a unique teahouse and an RV campground. This is a perfect location to use as a temporary headquarters and source of information; it is central to a number of nearby museums and also close to many historic sites in the district, some of which lack development.

About six kilometres northeast of the hamlet is Frenchman Butte National Historic Site, where the battle was fought. The historic site on the north side of the valley deals mainly with the Cree's defensive rifle pits. The militia did not construct any fortifications. There is a smaller monument dedicated to the militia on the south side of the ravine; however no one has taken on the responsibility of maintaining this particular site, which commemorates the last battle fought by Canadian troops on Canadian soil.

Some of the 1885 cart trails still exist, including the river trail followed by the Alberta Field Force east from Fort Pitt and the cart trail that crossed the valley through the Frenchman Butte battlesite. In places, the Carlton Trail is identified by small Red River cart signs, installed where the historic trail crosses existing roads, such as in the town of Paradise Hill. Portions of the wilderness trail used by the Cree to flee to Loon Lake are still used by all-terrain vehicles, but it is unmarked, despite its historic value.

The Loon Lake skirmish, as violent as it was, is not considered a battle. There is a small provincial historic park at the site, a marked grave of three of the defending Cree warriors and a hilltop viewpoint on the north side of the highway. From this elevated lookout are visible a sprinkling of white obelisks that identify where Cree warriors died defending their position on June 2, 1885.

The Alberta Field Force marched north to Cold Lake and Le Goff via Frog Lake as an occupying force just prior to the conclusion of the insurrection. Some of the troops camped beside Cold Lake, just south of the present Cold Lake Provincial Park boat launch. Today, virtually no one locally or in government is aware of the camp's existence. A similar situation exists with the Le Goff site, now a First Nations community.

In addition to the sites where Steele's Scouts saw action, there are several rebellion historic sites farther east in Saskatchewan, such as Cutknife Hill and Fort Battleford. Both have interpretive centres. Farther to the northeast is another interpretive centre at Duck Lake, near where the first battle occurred in March 1885. Tourond's Coulee features a monument and descriptive signs, while Batoche National Historic Site features the remains of the original community and battlefield, supported by a Metis-oriented interpretive centre. Batoche hosts several significant events during the summer months, drawing thousands of visitors to the site.

Sam Steele and his Scouts only operated for a short four-month period in the spring of 1885, but they still exist today in Calgary as an active re-enactment group that regularly appears in the Calgary Stampede parade, at Spruce Meadows Equestrian Centre and in various other events throughout the prairies. With over 100 members, this mounted, buckskin-clad group provides a colourful example of how the original Scouts would have appeared. For more information, go to www.steelescouts.ca.

The story of the rebellion is not complete without an understanding of the First Nations way of life following the uprising. Allen Sapp, a superb Cree artist from North Battleford, has poignantly portrayed life on the reserve in his paintings, which may be viewed at the Allen Sapp Gallery in North Battleford (www.allensapp.com/). Sapp conveys the heartbreaking, poverty-filled lifestyle foisted on the Cree and other First Nations by government bureaucracy.

Many details of the Northwest Rebellion remain to be discovered. Even today, after years of research, I occasionally encounter a tidbit of information resting in some obscure passage, which leads me to the revelation, "So that's the way it was!" I hope you enjoy your travels along the trail of 1885 as much as I have done.

Members of Steele's Scouts

The ranks of Steele's Scouts included 25 NWMP members, plus civilian scouts and Alberta Mounted Rifles who signed up in Calgary. Based on the initial handwritten Steele's Scouts roster, I've identified a total of 50 non-police inductees from Calgary. At least 19 more "cowboys" signed up along the way. The complete roster was tabled and recorded in the Canadian Parliamentary Sessional Papers of 1886 (44a) dated April 19, 1886, by Mr. Sproule, MP, but this document was lost in the 1916 Parliament Buildings fire. It is difficult to know the exact numbers with certainty.

Of note is the militia rank assigned to Steele and his NWMP members, required for military chain-of-command purposes. Steele was ranked as a major, sergeants retained their rank and most other Scouts were designated as troopers, although I've used their police ranks in the listing below. In addition, Parker and Chabot joined later in Edmonton, while other volunteers, including Sam's brothers Richard and Godfrey Steele, acted as message couriers as required and are not officially recognized as Scouts.

North West Mounted Police Members of Steele's Scouts
File # 3094 National Archives of Canada

Reg. # Service Dates

Major Samuel Benfield Steele	5	1873–1899
Sergeant William Fury	333	1879–1888
Sergeant William Parker	28	1874–1912
Corporal Alexander L. Davidson	523	1881–1886
Corporal Henry Gould	680	1882–1887

Members of Steele's Scouts

Corporal Albert McDonell	547	1881–1917
Corporal William. R. McMinn	549	1881–1887
Constable Ralph Bell	590	1881–1886
Constable John Bunt	975	1883–1890
Constable Joseph Chabot	474	1880–1885
Constable Thomas Craig	643	1882–1890
Constable Alexander Davidson	648	1882–1890
Constable Oscar Dubreuil	475	1880–1887
Constable Alexander Dyre	653	1882–1885
Constable Ernest Hall	684	1882–1886
Constable Samuel Hetherington	894	1883–1901
Constable George Jones	699	1882–1888
Constable Peter Kerr	704	1882–1888
Constable Donald McRae	716	1882–1887
Constable Robert Morton	719	1882–1887
Constable Ernest Percival	557	1881–1903
Constable Frederick Richardson	758	1882–1887
Constable John Robinson	759	1882–1887
Constable John Walters	795	1882–1888
Constable Thomas Waring	790	1882–1890
Constable James Whipps	784	1882–1887

Civilian Members of Steele's Scouts
Captain James K. Oswald, Commander

Calgary Inductees

Linas Ahlenias
John Alley
Thomas Anderson
R.L. Barber
Joseph Benoit
George Borradaille
Richard Broderick

Joseph Butlin
Edward Cole
John Corryell
William Fielders
Thomas James "Jumbo" Fisk
William Fisk
Joseph Garand

George Gouin
Edward Hayes
Watson Hunt
Charles Hurrell
William Huston
William Inglis
William Jardine
Samuel Kendig
William Lyne
Donald Macpherson
Reverend John McDougall
Robert McFarlane
William McKellar
William McManus
William McQuarrie
Frank Miller
William Murray
? Nash

William Oake
Frank Owen
W.F. Pew
Arthur Philipps
Edward F. Racey
James Rodgers
Charles Sanson
William Scott
William Simms
Albert Simons
Alexander Smith
Harry Smith
Louis Trepanier
Albert Welsh
William West
Milton Williams
Peter Young

Edmonton Inductees
John Beldon
J. Calder
"Doc" Thomas Edmonson
William Ibbleson
Reverend George McKay
    (joined en route)
Arthur Patton
James Petrie
Alexander Rowland
Fred Rowland

Walter Rowland
Wyndham Spearin
A.B. Spence
William Stiff
Frederick Walters
William West
George White
C. Whitford
John Whitford
L. Whitford

Timeline

July 8, 1874 The North West Mounted Police commence the Great March West from Fort Dufferin to Fort Whoop-Up.

August 23, 1876 Sam Steele attends the co-signing of Treaty 6 at Fort Carlton.

September 9, 1876 Sam Steele attends the co-signing of Treaty 6 at Fort Pitt.

July 1884 Louis Riel, back from exile in Montana, arrives at Batoche, Saskatchewan.

March 19, 1885 Louis Riel declares his provisional government at Batoche.

March 26, 1885 Superintendent Leif Crozier, commanding a force of NWMP and Prince Albert volunteers, confronts a Metis force led by Louis Riel and Gabriel Dumont at the Battle of Duck Lake.

March 29, 1885 A.P. Caron, minister of militia, requests retired General Thomas B. Strange to form the Alberta Field Force in Calgary.

April 2, 1885 Cree war chief Wandering Spirit leads a group of dissidents in murdering residents of the community of Frog Lake and taking a number of prisoners as hostages.

April 11, 1885 Sam Steele arrives in Calgary. He meets with General Strange and subsequently forms Steele's Scouts.

April 13, 1885 A large Cree force surrounds Fort Pitt in late afternoon.

April 14, 1885 William McLean begins negotiations with the Cree at Fort Pitt. An agreement is reached and the fort's civilians surrender to the Cree while the NWMP detachment of 25 flee downriver to Fort Battleford. Fort Pitt is sacked by the Cree during the night.

April 20, 1885 Steele's Scouts lead the Alberta Field Force out of Calgary on the trail to Edmonton.

April 25, 1885 Gabriel Dumont defends his position at Tourond's Coulee (Fish Creek) against General Frederick Middleton's military force. The battle ends in a draw.

May 1, 1885 Steele's Scouts and the rest of the Alberta Field Force march into Edmonton.

May 2, 1885 Colonel William Otter leads his mixed force of militia and NWMP on a pre-emptive attack on Chief Poundmaker's Cree camp at Cutknife Hill. They are forced to retreat after sustaining significant casualties.

May 6, 1885 Steele's Scouts begin ranging out, exploring east of Edmonton toward Victoria Settlement.

May 9, 1885 General Middleton's force marches on the Metis stronghold of Batoche and establishes positions.

May 12, 1885 Metis defences at Batoche collapse under a concerted attack led by Colonel Williams and his men, part of General Middleton's rebellion suppression force.

May 14, 1885 General Strange's flotilla of river scows cast off from the river landing at Edmonton and drift eastward on the North Saskatchewan River. Simultaneously, the land portion of the Alberta Field Force commences their march toward Victoria Settlement via the north branch of the Carlton Trail.

May 17, 1885 Steele's Scouts begin ranging out from Victoria Settlement and exploring to the east.

May 19, 1885 The Alberta Field Force departs from Victoria Settlement, the Winnipeg Light Infantry marching by the Carlton Trail and the 65th Mount Royal Rifles by river scow.

Timeline

May 24, 1885 The Alberta Field Force arrives at the Frog Lake community.

May 26, 1885 The Alberta Field Force arrives at Fort Pitt. Steele becomes involved in a midnight firefight with Cree warriors at Pipestone Creek.

May 28, 1885 The Alberta Field Force faces the dug-in defensive positions of the Cree at the Battle of Frenchman Butte. The fighting ends when both sides simultaneously retire.

June 1, 1885 Sam Steele leads the Scouts in pursuit of the Cree fleeing toward Loon Lake.

June 3, 1885 Steele's Scouts battle the Cree at Loon Lake in an attempt to free the prisoners. Both sides retire because of a lack of ammunition.

June 5, 1885 General Middleton's force withdraws from Loon Lake and marches overland via Frog Lake to follow General Strange.

June 18, 1885 The last prisoners are released by the Cree.

June 25, 1885 Rebellion suppression forces depart Le Goff Settlement to return to Fort Pitt.

June 29, 1885 The first contingent of troops depart Fort Pitt by paddlewheeler for home.

July 2, 1885 Chief Big Bear surrenders near Fort Carlton.

July 4, 1885 Steele's Scouts depart from Fort Pitt for home.

July 18, 1885 Steele and his Scouts arrive back in Calgary.

November 16, 1885 Louis Riel is hanged in Regina.

November 27, 1885 Wandering Spirit and five other Cree warriors are hanged at Fort Battleford.

Bibliography

Brown, Wayne. *Steele's Scouts*. Surrey, BC: Heritage House, 2001.

Cameron, William Bleasdell. *Blood Red the Sun*. Calgary: Kenway Publishing, 1926.

Degenstein, Barry. *The Pursuit of Louis Riel*. Saskatoon: Barry Degenstein, 2008.

Hoffman, Leslie and Edgar Mapletoft, contributors. *Fort Pitt History Unfolding*. Fort Pitt, SK: Fort Pitt Historical Society, 1985.

Light, Douglas. *Footprints in the Dust*. North Battleford: Turner-Warwick Publications Inc., 1987.

Loon Lake Historical Society. *The Loon Lake Story*. Loon Lake, SK: Loon Lake Historical Society, 1983.

McLean, Duncan, as told to Eric Wells. "The Last Hostage." *Weekend Magazine* 18, nos. 32–33 (1968).

Steele, Samuel B. *Forty Years on Canada*. New York: Dodd, Mead, 1915.

Stonechild, Blair and Bill Waiser. *Loyal till Death*. Calgary: Fifth House Ltd., 1997.

Index

Acknowledgements

With any book, the author is only the front man in the publishing process. A number of individuals provided me with enormous assistance and deserve recognition for the time and skills they contributed to the creation of this book.

First, I'm so very indebted to my old friend, the late Edgar Mapletoft. He was a warm-hearted, truly remarkable man who was instrumental in guiding and inspiring me to seek out our Western Canadian heritage. His favourite declaration still lingers in my mind: "Listen . . . You hear that awful squeaking way off? The ghost carts (Red River carts) are coming, they'll be here soon!" Edgar was a meticulous historian, an honorary elder of the Onion Lake Cree Nation and one of the founding members of the Frenchman Butte Museum. His dusty files, crammed with historic detail, rest in our museum's library. Only a small portion of his research has ever been published.

Second, I am grateful to my wife Marilyn, who also holds a deep interest in exploring our heritage. A faithful companion on field excursions, she possesses an intense desire to understand the historical incidents of our area. I also have the deepest appreciation for her willingness to employ her old schoolteacher skills in diligently critiquing and editing this story.

Finally, I'd like to express my appreciation to Heritage House editor Lesley Reynolds, who somehow endured grooming my graceless text into a pleasurable experience for readers.

I applaud the three of you and many unnamed others for your support.

About the Author

Wayne Brown grew up alongside the railway tracks in the coal-mining town of Drumheller, Alberta. After leaving Drumheller in 1967, he served for 30 years as a fish and wildlife officer in several areas of Alberta. Wayne's patrol duties inevitably carried him past historical sites where he'd spend a few moments savouring the story of each commemorative sign and surveying the area it described. In 1971, Wayne visited the major sites of the 1885 Northwest Rebellion and first thought of writing a book on the subject.

In 1998, after his retirement, Wayne and his wife, Marilyn, moved to their present home at Peck Lake in northwestern Saskatchewan, halfway between the 1885 battle sites of Frenchman Butte and Steele Narrows at Loon Lake. Wayne began to explore the nearby undisturbed sites of the rebellion and to research the stories of those who fought there. In the process, he uncovered many new and intriguing details about the events that occurred in 1885. Wayne is also a member of the Steele's Scouts Commemorative Militia Cavalry.